As a shrewd and entertaining interpreter of countries and peoples Dr. Capek, author of "The Gardener's Year" and "R.U.R.," has few equals. In the present volume he writes with humor and insight about Spain — about cities and buildings, flowers and vegetation, Goya and El Greco, foods and wines, women, flamencos, and of course, bull fights. His impressions have an extraordinary freshness exciting to those who know Spain as well as to the uninitiated. The chapters on bull fighting are particularly brilliant and throughout this leisurely and sparkling account runs Dr. Capek's own special wit. The volume is decorated with a wealth of drawings by the author which are even more confidential and expressive than his pleasant style.

"The delight of the week is Karel Capek's latest sheaf of travel sketches. 'Letters from Spain' . . . A glorious sun-drenched volume. A perfect present. . . ."—London *Daily Herald*.

"Charm and humor prevail. He gives us some of the best descriptions of a bull fight, and of the feelings of a spectator, that we have read."— London *Observer*.

LETTERS FROM SPAIN

LETTERS
FROM
SPAIN

By
KAREL ČAPEK

Translated by PAUL SELVER

G. P. PUTNAM'S SONS
NEW YORK
1932

PRINTED IN GREAT BRITAIN

CONTENTS

CONTENTS

Nord and Sud Express

IN recent times what are known as international expresses have become extremely important accessories to travel, partly on practical grounds, which are of minor interest to us, and partly for poetical reasons. Time after time in modern poetry the Transcontinental Express dashes past you, and a mysterious porter calls out the names of stations : Paris, Moscow, Honolulu, Cairo ; the Sleeping Cars dynamically scan the rhythm of Speed, and the Pullman, as it whirls by, suggests all the magic of distant places, for you must know that nothing less than first-class travel accommodation will satisfy the fine frenzy of the poet. My poetical friends, allow me to tell you the plain truth about Pullmans and Sleeping Cars : if you must know, they look infinitely more enticing from outside, when they flash past some sleepy little station, than from within. It is true that they make up for this by their tremendous speed, but it is no less true that all the same you are boxed up in them for fourteen or even twenty-three blessed hours at a stretch, and as a rule

that's enough to bore you stiff. A local train from Prague to Řepy jogs along at a less impressive speed, but at least you know that in half an hour you'll be able to get out and pursue some fresh adventure. A man in a Pullman car doesn't dash along at sixty miles an hour ; he just sits and yawns ; if the face on the right annoys him, he goes and sits down on the other side. The only redeeming feature of it is that he has a comfortable seat. Sometimes he gazes listlessly out of the window; a small station whisks past, and he can't read the name of it; a township flits by and he can't get out there; he'll never stroll along that road bordered with plane-trees, he'll never dawdle on that bridge and spit in the river—in fact he won't even find out what the river is called. Confound it all, thinks the man in the Pullman, where are we? What, only Bordeaux? Good Lord, this is a slow business!

Wherefore, if you want to have a trip with at least something exotic about it, get into a local train which puffs its way along from one wayside station to another. Press your nose against the window-pane, so as not to miss anything: here a soldier with a blue uniform gets in, here a child waves its hand at you; a French peasant in a black cowl lets you have a swill at his wine, a young mother gives her baby a breast as pale as moonlight, the country yokels hold forth noisily and smoke their shag, a snuff-stained priest says his breviary; the land unwinds, station after station, like the beads on a rosary. And then evening comes, when the jaded passengers doze like emigrants under the flickering lights. At that moment the lustrous International Express hurtles past on the other track with its load of weary boredom, with its Sleeping Cars and Dining Cars.

What's that, only Dax? Heavens above, what a tiresome journey!

9

Not long ago I read a eulogy of the Suit-case ; of course, not the common or garden suit-case, but the International Suit-case, plastered over with hotel labels from Constantinople and Lisbon, Tetuan and Riga, St. Moritz and Sofia ; the suit-case which is the pride of its owner, whose travels it records. I will reveal a dreadful secret to you : those labels are sold in travel agencies. For a moderate fee your suit-case will be labelled Cairo, Flushing, Bucharest, Palermo, Athens and Ostend.

With this revelation, I hope, I have inflicted a mortal wound in the International Suit-case.

It is possible that another man in my place, travelling all those thousands of miles, would meet with something different in the way of adventures ; perhaps he could come across the International Venus or the Madonna of the Sleeping Cars. Nothing of that sort happened to me ; there was only a collision, but I really couldn't help that. In some wayside station our express dashed into a goods train ; the contest was an

unequal one and the result of it was much the
same as if Mr. Chesterton had sat on somebody's
top-hat. The goods train fared very badly, while
on our side there were only five wounded ; it was
a thorough victory. When, in such a contin-
gency, a passenger has wriggled out from under-
neath a suit-case which has fallen on his head, he
first of all rushes off to see what has happened ;
not until he has satisfied his curiosity does he
begin to fumble about to discover whether he has
any bones broken. When he has made sure that,
roughly speaking, he is sound in wind and limb,
he derives a certain amount of technical pleasure
in observing how the two engines have got
rammed together and what a thorough mess we
have made of the goods train ; well, it oughtn't
to have interfered with us. Only the injured
passengers are pale and rather disgruntled, as if
a personal and unjust humiliation has been
inflicted upon them. Then the authorities poke
their noses into it and we go off to drink to our
victory in the remnants of the dining-car. For
the rest of the journey they leave us a free passage,
we have evidently put the fear of God into them.

Another and a more complicated adventure is
how to get into the upper berth in a sleeping-car,
especially when someone is already asleep in the
lower one. It is somewhat disconcerting to
trample on the head and abdomen of a person
whose nationality and character are alike unknown
to you. There are various wearisome methods of

getting on top : by such physical jerks as the upward stretch, with or without a preliminary jump,

by vaulting, by straddling, by fair means or foul.
Once you are up there, make sure not to get
thirsty or anything of that sort which would
involve climbing down ; surrender yourself into
the hands of God, and try to sleep like a corpse
in a coffin, while unknown and strange regions
are whizzing past outside, and at home poets are
writing verses about International Expresses.

D. R., *Belgique, France*

IF I were wealthy enough, and if such things were for sale in the open market, I should certainly start making a collection of countries. I have discovered that frontiers are by no means to be despised, although I am not fond of customs

PROVINZ BRANDEBURG

officers, and passport inspections bore me. I nevertheless notice with a delight which is always fresh that when I cross the frontiers from one country to another, I penetrate into a new world, with different houses and a different language, different policemen, a different colour of the soil and different scenery. A blue railway-guard is replaced by a green one who, in his turn, a few hours later, will make way for a brown one. Really, it's just like the Arabian Nights. Czech apple-trees are followed by the fir-trees of Brandenburg on white stretches of sand, a windmill waves its arms as if it were running away, the country-side is neatly levelled out and produces chiefly advertisements of cigarettes and margarine.

Then rocks covered with ivy, hills which have been hollowed out by mining operations, deep green river-basins, the forges and foundries of steel-works, the iron ribs of pithead towers, slag-heaps which look like recently extinguished vol-

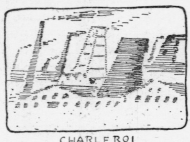

CHARLEROI

canoes, a medley of rustic scenery and heavy industry, a concerto in which the shawm and the carillon accompany the factory siren : Verhaeren in his entirety, *Les heures claires* as well as *Les villes tentaculaires*. The whole of Flanders as the old poet portrayed it : the country which has not found enough room for its treasures and keeps them all in one pocket ; winsome Belgium ; a mother with her baby in her arms, a young soldier watering a horse, an inn at the bottom of a hill, the chimney-stacks and formidable towers of industry, a Gothic church and an iron-foundry,

some cows among the mine-shafts—all these
things neatly arranged like objects in an old-
fashioned shop—heaven alone knows how room
has been found for them.

Ah, but now there is more elbow-room. This
is France, the country of alders and poplars,
poplars and plane-trees, plane-trees and vineyards. Silvery green, yes, a green silveriness is
the colour of it ; pink bricks and blue slates ; a

ORLÉANAIS

slight veil of mist, more light than colour, Corot.
Not a mortal soul in the fields ; perhaps they are
pressing the grape-crops, the gladsome wine of
Touraine, the gladsome wine of Anjou ; Balzac's
goodly wine and the wine of Monsieur le Comte
de la Fère. *Garçon, une demi-bouteille* and here's
to you, turrets of the valley of the Loire ! Black-
haired women dressed in black. What, only Bordeaux ? Resinous fragrances are wafted on the
night air ; here are the Landes, the region of
pine-trees. Then a different fragrance, keen and
exhilarating : the sea.

Hendaye, all change ! An official with the face of a young Caligula in a shiny three-cornered hat scrawls a magic sign on the luggage, and with a lordly gesture ushers us on to the platform. Well, so far, so good : I am in Spain.

Camerero, una media de jerez. So far, so good. A devilish fine Spanish girl, her fingers dyed with henna. Now then, keep away from there. All the same, I wish I could take that official, as a stuffed specimen, home with me !

Castilla la Vieja

YES, I have been in Spain ; I can swear most solemnly to that, and I have a number of witnesses to prove it, e.g. the hotel-labels on my suit-case. And yet as far as I am concerned, the land of Spain is shrouded with an impenetrable mystery, for the sound reason that I entered it and left it again at dead of night ; it was just as if we had been taken blindfold across the River Acheron or through the Mountains of Dreams. I tried to distinguish something in the darkness outside ; I saw something that looked like a cluster of black patches on the bare hill-sides ; perhaps they were rocks or trees, but they might also have been large animals. The mountains were severe and strange of aspect ; I decided that I could get up early to have a look at them at day-break. I did get up early ; according to the map and the time-table we ought to have been somewhere in the mountains, but all I saw below the red streak of daybreak was a brown, bare and frowning expanse ; it looked like the sea or a mirage. I thought I must be feverish, for I had never seen a plain like that before ; so I went to sleep again, and when I woke up once more and looked out of the window, I discovered that I was not feverish, but that I was in a different land and that land was Africa.

I do not know how to put it; there is a green tint here, but it is different from ours; it is dim and drab. There is a brown tint, but it is different from ours; it is not the brown tint of ploughed earth, but the brown tint of stony land and powdered lignite. There are red rocks here, but there is something stagy about their redness.

CASTILLA LA VIEJA

And there are mountains too, which are fashioned, not of rock, but of deep clay and boulders. These boulders do not sprout out of the soil; they look as if they had been showered down on to it. The mountains are called Sierra de Guadarama; God, who created them, must be very mighty, or how else could He have made so many stones? Among the boulders grow dark oaks and besides them scarcely anything but wild thyme and thorns. It is bare and large, as parched as a desert, as mysterious as Sinai; I do not quite

18

know how to express my meaning, but it is another continent, it is not Europe. It is sterner and fiercer than Europe ; it is older than Europe. It is not a mournful wilderness ; it is solemn and strange, rough and majestic. People dressed in black, black goats, black pigs against a background of torrid russet. A harsh existence, scorched to blackness among the heated stones.

Here and there the bare boulders are streams,

the bare stones form a plain and the bare stone walls a Castillian pueblo. An angular tower and a wall around ; it is more of a stronghold than a village. It is welded together with the stony soil, just as old castles are welded together with the rock on which they stand. The huts are huddled one against the other, as if they were awaiting an attack. This then is a Spanish village. The human dwellings blend with the stony earth.

And in the brown, stony slope there is a miracu-

lous sight : dark green gardens, avenues of dark
cypresses, a dense and gloomy park ; a huge,
stark and lordly cube with four bristling turrets ;

a monumental solitude, a hermitage with a thousand haughty windows : El Escorial. The cloister
of the Spanish kings. A castle of sorrow and
pride above the parched country-side, where meek
asses graze.

Puerta del Sol

OH yes, I know that here I ought to discuss many other matters, such as the history of Madrid, the view on the Manzanares, the gardens in Buen Retiro, the royal palace with the guardsmen in red and the shouting bevy of pretty children in the courtyard, a whole lot of churches and museums and the other main sights. If it interests you, please read it up elsewhere ; all I offer you is Puerta del Sol, and just as a special favour to you, I will add Calle de Alcalá and Calle Mayor, together with the tepid evenings and all the people of Madrid.

There are sacred places in the world ; they are the most beautiful streets in the world, the beauty of which is as irrational and mysterious as a myth. There is the Cannebière in Marseilles ; there is the Rambla in Barcelona ; there is the Alcalá in Madrid. If you were to detach them from their surroundings, boiling them down and depriving them of their life and all their small local odours, and then put them elsewhere, you would not notice anything remarkable about them ; why, you would say, this is quite a nice wide street, but what else is there ? What else, O ye of little faith ? Don't you see that this square is sacred, nay more, that the world-renowned Puerta del

Sol, the Gate of the Sun, is the centre of the world and the navel of Madrid? Don't you see how this priest, more dignified and stately than any other priest in the world, is wending his way along, with his cloak tucked up beneath his arm like a soldier with a rolled great-coat. And here, this Spanish hidalgo, disguised as a gendarme in a

shiny hat dented at the back; another caballero, probably a marquis or something of that sort, with an aquiline nose and the voice of a crusader leading his warriors, is shouting *El Sooól* or the name of some other newspaper; and here again is a conquistador, leaning on a broom, and with sculptural gestures performing an allegory of some kind, perhaps the Cleansing of the City. But

here are some pleasant people : lean and sun-
burnt peasants from the Sierras, bringing veget-
ables and melons with them on the backs of
donkeys ; enough red, blue and green uniforms
to mount a dozen decorative ballets ; limpiabotas
with their small stands——

Wait a bit : this is a chapter all to itself and
headed : boot-cleaning. The cleaning of boots
is a national Spanish trade ; or in exacter terms,
the cleaning of boots is a national Spanish dance

or ceremony. In other parts of the world, Naples,
for instance, a bootblack will hurl himself upon
your footwear furiously, and will start brushing
it as if he were conducting the experiment in
physics, by which heat or electricity is produced
as the result of friction. Spanish boot-cleaning
is a dance, which, like the Siamese dances, is performed only with the hands. The dancer kneels
down before you as a sign that this performance
is being held in honour of Your Lordship ; with
an elegant movement he turns up your trousers,
with a graceful pass he smears the respective foot-

wear with a fragrant salve or something of that sort, whereupon he indulges in a frenzied set of dancing movements ; he flings the brush upwards, seizes it again, slaps it across from one hand to the other, allowing it to touch your boots in a respectful and flattering manner. The meaning of this dance is clear : it expresses respect ; you are a magnificent grandee, receiving the ceremonious homage of a knightly page. Accord-

ingly, a magnificent and agreeable warmth, mounting from the feet, spreads inside you ; which is certainly worth half a peseta.

Oiga, camerero, una copita de Fundador. You know, *caballeros*, this has quite taken my fancy : all this crowd, this noise, which is not an uproar, the gay courtesy, the charm ; all of us are cavaliers, tramp and custodian of the law, I and the crossing-sweeper, we are all of noble birth, wherefore long live southern equality ! *Madrileñas*, you handsome long-nosed women in black mantillas with

your dark optics, with what dignity do you bear yourselves in your half-concealment ; senoritas with dark-eyed mamas, mamas and their babies with small round pates, like dolls ; fathers who are not ashamed of their love for their children, old women with rosaries, good-humoured fellows with the faces of brigands, beggars, gentlemen with gold teeth, pedlars, caballeros one and all ; a bright and bustling crowd which chats and strolls in a good-tempered allegro.

But the evening comes, the air is steeped in warmth and has a keen savour ; the whole of Madrid, if it has legs at all, is walking, thronging and surging from Calle Mayor as far as Calle de Alcalá ; caballeros in uniforms, caballeros in plain clothes, in sombreros and caps, girls of all denominations, viz. madamiselas, doncellas and muchachas, señoritas and mozas and chulas, madamas and señoras, dueñas, dueñazas and dueñisimas, hijas, chicas, chiquitas and chiquir-riticas with dark eyes behind the dark mantilla, with red lips, red finger-nails and dark side-glances, all promenading, a festival of workaday, a processional demonstration of amorous and flirtatious charm, a pleasaunce of eyes, an avenue of endless erotic enchantment.

Cannebière, Rambla, Alcalá : the most delight-ful streets in the world ; streets which overflow with life, like a goblet with wine.

Toledo

YOU have here a brown, warm plain, studded with villages, donkeys, olives and dome-shaped walls ; from this plain, without any warning, a great granite rock thrusts itself, and all the objects on it are squeezed together, one on top of the other ; and below in the chasm of brown rocks flows the brown Tajo.

As regards Toledo itself, I really don't know whether to begin with the ancient Romans or the Moors or the Catholic Kings. But as Toledo is a mediaeval town, I will begin with what a mediaeval town undoubtedly begins with, viz. the gates. For instance, Toledo has a gate known as Bisagra nueva, rather in the style of Terezín, with a Habsburg double eagle which is distinctly above life-size ; it looks as if it led to our Terezín or Josefov, but contrary to all expectation it debouches into a quarter which is called Arrabál and looks it, too. Whereupon you are in front of another gate which is called the Gate of the Sun, and looks as if you had been set down in Bagdad, but instead of that the Moorish portal leads into the streets of the most Catholic of towns, where every third building is a church with a bloodstained Jesus and an ecstatic retable

27

of Greco. Also you wander through winding Arab by-streets, gaze through gratings into Moorish courtyards which are called patios and are inlaid with Toledan majolica, you keep clear of donkeys laden with wine or oil, you peep at the beautiful harem-gratings of the windows and altogether you trudge along as if in a dream. As if in a dream. You might come to a standstill at every seventh step ; here is a Visigoth pillar and there a Mozareb wall ; here a miraculous Virgin Mary, who finds a wife or a husband for all, and

there a Mudejar minaret and renaissance palace like a fortress, and Gothic windows, and a façade encrusted with gold and gems in the estilo plateresco, and a mosque, and a street so narrow that a donkey can only get through if he squeezes his ears back ; glimpses of shady majolica courtyards where fountains gurgle amid flower-pots ; glimpses of serried streets between bare walls and barred windows ; glimpses of the sky ; glimpses of churches frantically decorated with everything which can be carved, hewn, moulded, damascened, hammered, painted, embroidered, tricked

28

out with filigree, gilded and set with precious
stones. Thus you can stop at every step, as in
a museum ; or you can walk along as in a dream,
for all this, the products of a thousand years,
marked with the flaming script of Allah, the cross
of Christ, the gold of the Incas, the life of diverse

periods, gods, civilizations, and races, is, after all,
a fantastically uniform thing ; so many periods
and civilizations enter the hard clutch of the
Toledan rock. And then, in one of the narrowest
streets, from the barred window of a human cage
a bird's-eye view of Toledo is revealed to you :
one single surge of flat roofs beneath the blue

sky : an Arab town, glistening in the brown rocks, gardens on the roofs, and delightful, languorous patios with an intimate and comely life of their own.

But if I were to take you by the hand and show you over everything that was revealed to me in Toledo, I suppose I should first lose my way in those winding poverty-stricken streets. Not that I should regret that, for there too we should have to keep clear of the donkeys, pattering over the cobbles with their nimble hoofs, we should see the open patios and the majolica staircases and moreover we should encounter people. Perhaps here I should find that Mudejar chapel, white and chilly, with its fine horse-shoe arches ; a little further on is a rock which falls sheer into the Tajo, and opens out a magnificent and austere vista ; and the synagogue del Transito, bestrewn with fragile and curiously refined Moorish ornamentation. And churches : thus, the one with Greco's " Burial of the Count Orgaz," or the one with that magnificent Moorish cloister, just like a dream. And the hospitals with palatial court-yards. There is one of them in front of the gate, and in it there are poor nuns with huge wing-shaped headgear and a crowd of orphans holding hands, like a long snake, as they trudge along to church singing " Antonino " or " Santo niño " or something of that sort ; and for their use there is an old dispensary with beautifully enamelled pots and flagons labelled : " Divinus Quercus "

or " Caerusa," " Sagapan " or " Spica Celtic,"
remedies that have stood the test of time.

Now concerning the cathedral, I am not sure
whether I was there or not ; for as just in front
of it I sampled the Toledan wine, wine from the
Vega plain, a drop of wine so liquid that it flows
down the throat all by itself, and a wine as thick
as a curative oil, I am not prepared to swear that
I did not dream about it or muddled it up some-

how. There was too much of it ; I know that
there were exquisite miniatures and fantastic
ciboria, gratings which reached to the skies,
carved retables with a thousand statues, jasper
balustrades, canonical chairs carved from above,
from below, from the middle and from the back,
pictures by Greco, organs rumbling in some place
unknown, prebendaries as stout and desiccated as
stockfish, chapels inlaid with marble, painted
chapels, black chapels, golden chapels, Turkish

banners, canopies, angels, tapers and vestments, impassioned Gothic and impassioned Baroque, plateresque altars and a churriguesque Transparency absurdly bulging beneath a dark, lofty, vaulted dome, a medley of senseless and amazing things, of glowing lights and awe-inspiring darkness—well, perhaps I only dreamt about it; perhaps it was only a dreadful, confused dream in the wicker chair of the church, perhaps it is not even possible for any religion to need all these things.

So, caballero, go for a stroll in the streets of Toledo to clear your head of this gluttonous wallowing in works of art. You, shapely windows, small Gothic arches, Gothic and Moorish *ajimez*; you, hammered *rejas*, houses with battlements, patios with children and palm trees, tiny courtyards inlaid with *azulejos*, streets of Moors, Jews and Christians, where it is a joy to loiter in the shadow, caravans of donkeys—in you, I say, and in many, many tiny details there is just as much history as in any cathedral, the best museum is the street of living people. I had almost said that here you imagine yourself straying into another age, but that is not true. The truth is stranger; there is no other age; what was, is. And if this caballero were begirded with a sword, and that priest yonder were to expound the scriptures of Allah, and that girl were the Jewess of Toledo, it would not strike you as being a whit more curious and remote than the walls of the Toledan streets. If I were to enter another age it would not be another age; it would be only a bewilderingly fine and high adventure. Like Toledo. Like the Spanish land.

Posada de la Sangre

THE Tavern at the sign of the Blood. It was here that Don Miguel de Cervantes Saavedra lived, drank, ran into debt and wrote his " Exemplary Tales." In Seville there is another inn, where he also drank and wrote, and a prison where he served a sentence for debt ; to-day, however, this prison is a tavern. On the basis of my own investigations I can prove to all and sundry that, while he drank Manzanilla and crunched langostinos with it in Seville, he treated himself to Toledan wine in Toledo and did justice to the chorizo with paprika and the jamon Serrano or black raw ham and other things which accompanied it, and which promote thirst, talent and eloquence. Until this very day Toledan wine is drunk from flagons and chorizo is munched in the Posada de la Sangre, while in the yard the caballeros unharness the donkeys and bandy jokes with the girls, just as they used to do at the time of Don Miguel. Which only shows the genius of Cervantes is unfading.

But while we are in the tavern, oiga, viajero ; you must eat and drink your way through distant countries, to get to know them properly ; and the more distant the countries are, the more, under

God, must you eat and drink your fill. And you will discover that all the nations of the world, down to the Saxons and Brandenburgers, have sought by sundry ways and means, as well as by sundry spices and processes, to achieve paradise

on earth ; wherefore they set to work baking, brazing and pickling the most diverse foods so as to achieve temporal bliss. Every nation has its own tongue, and indeed its own daintiness of tongue. Get to know its tongue ; eat its foods and drink its wines. Attune yourself whole-heartedly to the harmonies of its fish and cheeses, its oil and smoked meats and bread and fruit, amid the orchestral accompaniment of its wines, which are as numerous as musical instruments. There are wines as penetrating as a Basque reed-pipe, as harsh as *vendas*, as deep as guitars ; so

play your tunes to the wanderer, ye warm and sonorous wines ! *A la salud de Usted*, Don Miguel ! As you see, I am a foreigner ; I have crossed three countries to get here, but perhaps I could make friends with you all the same. Good, pour me out some more. You know, you Spaniards have a number of things in common with us Czechs ; for example, you have the same *ch* as we have, and our fine, hearty *rrr*, and you are fond of diminutives, just as we are ; *a la salud de Usted*. You ought to pay a visit to our country, Mr. Cervantes ; we would drink to your health in beer with white froth, and we would pile up your plate with other foods than these, for each nation has its own tongue, but we can make ourselves understood where sound and fundamental matters are concerned, such as a good tavern, realism, the arts and freedom of the spirit. *A la salud.*

Velázquez o la Grandeza

IF you want Velázquez you must go to Madrid, for one thing because most of his pictures are there, and then too, that is just the place, with its pomp in a sober setting, amid princely ostentation and plebeian hubbub, that city which is at once ardent and cold, where he seems to fit in almost as a matter of course. If I were to sum up Madrid briefly, I should say that it is a city of courtly show and fitful revolutions ; just notice how the people here hold their heads : it is half grandeza and half doggedness. If I have any flair at all for cities and people, I should say that in the atmosphere of Madrid there is something like a gentle tension which causes a slight excitement, while Seville blissfully takes its ease, and Barcelona seethes in semi-concealment.

Thus, Diego Velázquez de Silva, knight of Calatrava, royal marshal and court painter of that pale, cold and strange Philip IV, belongs to the Madrid of the Spanish Kings by a twofold right. First and foremost he has grandeur ; he is so supreme that he is beyond all lies. But this is not the exuberant, golden grandeur of Tizian ; there is in it a trenchant coldness, a delicate and yet unrelenting sense of detail, an uncanny sureness of eye and brain which rules the hand. I imagine that his king made him marshal, not to reward him, but because he feared him: because the intent and penetrating eyes of Velázquez made him uneasy: because he could not bear this

equality with the painter and he therefore raised him to the rank of grandee. So then it was a Spanish paladin who painted the pale king with the weary eyelids and frozen eyes, or the pale infantas with rouge on their faces, poor, tightly laced puppets. Or the court dwarfs with the dropsical heads, the palace jesters and fools, swaggering with grotesque dignity, a crippled and imbecile plebeian monstrosity unwittingly travestying the grandeur of the court. The king and

La grandeza

his dwarf, the court and its jester : Velázquez accentuated this antithesis too markedly and too consistently for it not to have its peculiar meaning. The royal marshal would scarcely paint the court menials if he himself did not wish to. If there were nothing more in it than this, then at least there is one cruel and cold-blooded message : this is the king and the world he lives in. Velázquez was too superb a painter merely to fulfil commissions ; and too great a man to paint only what he saw. He saw too well not to allow his eyes to serve as a medium of vision for the whole of his clear and supreme intelligence.

El Greco o la Devocion

YOU must search for Domenica Theotocopuli, known as El Greco, in Toledo ; not that he fits in there more than anything else, but the place is full of him and, besides, in Toledo nothing surprises you ; not even El Greco. A Greek by origin, a Venetian in colour, he was Gothic in his art, and by a whim of history he cropped up when Baroque was let loose. Imagine Gothic verticalism which has encountered a blast from a Baroque whirlwind ; the Gothic line warps, and a surge of Baroque darts up and permeates the perpendicular eruption of Gothic ; at times it seems as if the pictures were cracking with the tension of these two forces. There is such an impact that it distorts the faces, warps the bodies and flings garments upon them in heavy tempestuous folds ; clouds uncoil like bed-linen fluttering in a tempest, and through them penetrates an abrupt and tragical light, enkindling colours with an unnatural and eerie intensity. As if judgment-day had come, when signs and tokens are revealed in heaven and on earth.

And just as in Greco himself two types of form merge into each other, so also you feel in his pictures two conflicting elements which goad each

other on to extreme lengths : a direct and pure
vision of God, such as hallowed art up to the
Gothic period, and a rampant mysticism by which
the human, all-too-human Catholic Baroque was
emotionally stimulated. The old Christ was not
the Son of Man but God Himself in His glory.

Theotocopuli the Byzantine carried the old Christ
within him ; but in Baroque Europe he discovered
the humanized Christ who had been made flesh.
The old God held sway sublimely, relentlessly
and a little rigidly in his mandorla ; the Baroque
and Catholic God amid his angel choirs glided
to earth in order to clutch at the believer, and

draw him within the curving range of his glories. Greco the Byzantine came from the basilicas of holy silence into the churches with their loud surges of organ music and frenzied processions ; I should have imagined that this meant rather a lot to him ; but amid the uproar he did not lose the thread of his own prayers, and he himself began to shout in a dire and unnatural voice. In him there developed what might be called a frenzy of belief ; this mundane and material tumult did not assuage him ; he had to shout it down with a more shrill and vehement outcry. How odd : this eastern Greek surmounted western Baroque by raising it to an ecstatic pitch of emotion and getting rid of its exuberant and muscular human attributes. The older he grew, the more did he dehumanize the figures, lengthening the bodies out of all proportion, emaciating the faces with the gauntness of martyrdom, and fixing the eyes with a wide-open stare upon a pillar. Up, heavenward ! He removes reality from colours ; his darkness hisses and his colours are enkindled as if illuminated by lightning. Hands which are too fragile and incorporeal are uplifted in amazement and terror, the stormy heavens are rent asunder and the shrill lament of awe and belief reaches the ancient God.

Yes, this Greek was an overwhelming genius ; some assert that he was mad. Every man whose eyes become feverishly fixed upon his own visions is a little mad ; or at least he lapses into mannerisms because he takes from himself and from nowhere else the material and form of his visions. In Toledo foreigners are shown la Casa de Greco ; I cannot believe that this charming little house with the trim, tiled garden belonged to the queer Greek. It has too mundane a smile for that, and it also looks too prosperous. We know that the only heritage which Greco left to his son was two hundred of his pictures. Evidently at that time there was no very brisk demand for the retables of the eccentric Cretan. It is only to-day that the spectators crowd round these pictures in devout admiration ; but they are people without faith, who are in no way startled by the shrill and despairing outcry of the Greek's piety .

Goya o el Reverso

IN the Prado at Madrid there are dozens of
pictures and hundreds of drawings by him ;
and so for the sake of Goya, if for nothing else,
Madrid is a great place for a pilgrimage. Neither
before nor after him was there a painter who
pounced upon his age with so ample a clutch,
with such intense and ruthless verve, and portrayed it, seamy side and all ; Goya is not realism,
Goya is onslaught ; Goya is revolution ; Goya is
a pamphleteer multiplied by a Balzac.

His most exquisite work : designs for gobelins.
A rustic fair, children, paupers, an open-air dance,
an injured bricklayer, a brawl, girls with a jug,
a vintage, a snow-storm, games, a working-class
wedding ; sheer life, its joys and sorrows, playful
and evil scenes, a solemn and also a blissful
spectacle ; such teeming life, as lived by the
people, had never before surged forth in any cycle
of paintings. It produces the effect of a folk-
song, a frisky *jota*, a winsome *seguidilla* ; it is a
specimen of rococo, but now quite humanized ;
it is painted with a particular delicacy and relish
which is surprising in so fierce a painter as this.
Such is his attitude towards the people.

Portraits of the royal family : Carlos IV,

bloated and listless, like a bumptious, dull-witted jack-in-office ; Queen María Luisa, with rabid and gimlety eyes, an ill-favoured harridan and an arrant virago, their family bored, brazen and repulsive. Goya's portraits of kings are not far short of insults. Velázquez did not flatter ;

Goya went as far as to laugh Their Highnesses to scorn. It was ten years after the French Revolution, and a painter, without turning a hair, told the throne what he thought of it.

But a few years later there was another revolution : the Spanish nation flung itself tooth and nail upon the French conquerors. Two astounding pictures by Goya : a desperate attack by the Spaniards on Murat's mamelukes, and the execution of the Spanish rebels. These are specimens of reporting, which for sheer genius and emotional eloquence, have not their equal in the whole history of painting ; at the same time Goya, as a mere incidental, achieved that modernity of composition which was adopted by Manet sixty years later.

Maja desnuda : the modern revelation of sexuality. A barer and more carnal nudity than any which had preceded it. The end of erotic pretence. The end of allegorical nudity. It is the only nude by Goya, but there is more exposure in it than in tons of academic flesh.

Pictures from Goya's house : it was with this appalling witches' sabbath that the artist decorated his house. It consists almost entirely of mere black and white paintings feverishly flung on to the canvas ; it is like hell illuminated with livid flashes of lightning. Sorceresses, cripples and monstrosities : man in his dark wallowings and his bestiality. You might say that Goya turned man inside out, peering through his nostrils and his yawning gullet, studying his misshapen vileness in a distorting mirror. It is like a nightmare, like a shriek of horror and protest. I cannot imagine that this caused Goya any amusement : he more likely struggled frenziedly against some of it. I had an uneasy feeling that the horns of the Catholic devil and the cowls of the inquisitors protrude from this hysterical inferno. At that time the constitution had been abolished in Spain and the Holy Officium restored ; from the convulsions of the civil wars and with the help of the fanaticized mob the dark and bloody reaction of despotism had been installed. Goya's chamber of horrors is a ferocious shout of disgust and hatred. No revolutionary ever affronted the world with so frantic and virulent a protest.

El reverso

Goya's sketches : the feuilletons of a tremendous journalist. Scenes from life in Madrid, weddings and customs of the lower classes, *chulas* and beggars, the very essence of life, the very essence of the people ; *Los Toros*, bull-fights in their chivalrous aspect, their picturesque beauty, their blood and cruelty. The Inquisition, a fiendish church mummery, fierce and caustic pages from a lampoon ; *Desastres de la guerra*, a fearful indictment of war, a document for all time, pity which is truculent and ferocious in its passionate directness ; *Caprichos*, Goya's wild outbursts of laughter and sobbing at the hapless, ghastly and fantastic creature which arrogates an immortal soul to itself.

Reader, let me tell you that the world has not yet done justice to this great painter, this most modern of painters ; it has not yet learnt the lesson he teaches. This harsh and aggressive outcry, this violent and thrilling quintessence of mankind ; no academic dullness, no aesthetic trifling ; when a man can " see life steadily and see it whole," *really* see it, I mean, then he is the doer of deeds, he is a fighter, an arbiter, a fire-brand. There is a revolution in Madrid : Francisco Goya y Lucientes is erecting barricades in the Prado.

Y los Otros

THERE is nothing more I can marvel at ; after Goya I cannot stand in amazement before any of the masters, light or dark. Ribera is one of those dark and stern painters ; I like his gaunt old men and sinewy fellows to whom he gives the names of saints and martyrs ; but here is a holier master, half earthly and half redeemed, black as a cowl and white as an ironed surplice, and that is Zurbarán ; his name is broad and sturdy like his painting. All his life he painted friars ; they are lanky or haggard fellows, but they are always wrought of tough fibre ; they show what staunch discipline, what genuine, austere manliness formed the underlying ideas of monkhood. If you would see a glorification of man in his bony, bristly aspect, in his uncouth, unshaven condition, do not search for the portraits of army leaders or kings, but look at the great monks of the worthy and pious Zurbarán.

And if you want to see Murillo, it is better to go to Seville ; you will discover that what makes his work so attractive is its amorous Sevillan tenderness. His Holy Virgins in a soft, warm light—why, they are the lush girls of Seville, proud and winsome damsels : and Don Esteban, good man that he was, glorified the heavens by discovering heaven in Andalusia. He also painted pretty, curly-haired boys from Triana or one of the suburbs ; to-day these pictures of boys are scattered in museums all over the world, but those

ZURBARAN o os frailes

boys themselves are in Spain to this very day and they roam about in all paseos and plazas making a terrific, hearty din ; and when they spy a foreigner looking for the children of Murillo, they rush round him uttering a war-cry, and extort pesetas and perros from him in the un-abashed and traditional mendicant manner of southern children.

MURILLO o los niños

And now, when I take stock of Spanish art as a whole ; when I recall the wax Christs and polychrome statues with all the appurtenances of the tortured and flayed body ; the tombs which make you almost smell the actual odour of decay ; the misshapen and relentless portraits—heavens above, what a peepshow ! Spanish art has almost made a special point of displaying man as he is, with terrible emphasis and almost in a declamatory manner : Behold, this is Don Quixote ! Behold, this is a king ! Behold, this is a cripple ! Lo, such is man ! Perhaps this is the Catholic denial of our sinful and mortal bodily husk ; perhaps it is——

Wait a moment, I must now add something about the Moors. You cannot conceive what artists they were ; their upholstery, their tints, the architectural filigree and arched doorways, what magic and brilliance, what delicacy, what feverish creativeness, what proficiency in the plastic arts ! But the Koran forbade them to portray man ; they were not allowed to imitate man or create idols in his image. It was the Christian re-conquest of Spain which, together with the cross, brought the image of man. It is perhaps since then, perhaps because the curse of the Koran was broken, that the image of man has occupied Spanish art so intensely and sometimes even preposterously. Up to the nineteenth century, Spain, vastly picturesque though it is, has no landscape painting ; only images of man, of man on a wooden cross, of man in the height of his power, of man the cripple, of man dead and in decay . . . until the apocalyptic democracy of Francisco de Goya y Lucientes.

Andalucía

I MUST frankly admit that when I woke up in the train and looked through the window, I hadn't the faintest idea where I was ; alongside the railway-line I saw something that looked like a quickset hedge, behind it brown, flat fields, and from them protruded, here and there, sparse and jaded-looking trees. I had a strong and comfort-

able impression that I was travelling somewhere between Bratislava and Nové Zámky, and I began to give myself a wash and brush up, lustily whistling " Kysúca, Kysúca " and other songs appropriate to the occasion. When, however, I had exhausted my supply of Czech songs I perceived that what I had taken for a quickset hedge was a dense aftergrowth of opuntia, six feet high, plump aloes and a sort of stunted palm-tree, probably chamaerops, and the jaded trees were, I found, date-palms, while the brown tilled plain was apparently Andalusia.

So you see how it is ; if you were travelling

across the tilled pampas, the Australian maize-fields, the wheat-laden expanses of Canada, or heavens knows where else, it would be exactly like the country near Kolín or Břeclav. Nature is infinitely various, and as regards man, he differs in hair, language and a thousand sundry ways of life ; but the farmer's work is the same every-where, and arranges the face of the earth in the same straight and regular furrows. The houses are different, and so are the churches ; why, even the telegraph poles are different in each country, but the tilled field is the same everywhere, whether in the neighbourhood of Pardubice or of Seville. There is something great and also a trifle monotonous about this.

But I must add that the farmer of Andalusia has not the same broad and clumsy gait as ours; the Andalusian farmer rides on a donkey, which makes him look excessively Biblical and droll.

Calles Sevillanas

I WAGER a bottle of aljarafe, or anything you like, that every guide, every journalist, and even every young lady tourist, will refer to " smiling " Seville. Certain stock phrases and epithets possess the ghastly and irritating quality of being right. You can knock me down or call me a purveyor of tushery or an arrant babbler for saying so, but " smiling " Seville really is smiling Seville. Nothing can be done about it ; in fact, there is no other way of describing the place. It is just " smiling " Seville ; in every corner of its eyes and mouth there is a flutter of merriment and tenderness.

And perhaps it is only that a street, however narrow, glistens as if it were freshly whitewashed every Saturday. And that from every window, from every lattice in it are thrust garlands, pelargonia and fuchsias, small palms and all kinds of greenery, blossoming and leafy. Here the awnings have still remained from the summer, stretched from roof to roof, and intersected by the sky, as by a blue knife ; and when you stroll along, you seem to be, not in the street, but in the flower-laden passage of a house where you are paying a visit ; at this corner somebody may perhaps shake you by the hand and say : " We *are* pleased to see you " or " ¿ Qué tal ? " or something cheerful of that sort. And everything here is as clean as a new pin ; there is a smell of garlands and frying oil ; every door with its lattice leads to a trim heavenly garden which is called a patio, and here again is a church with a majolica dome and a portal as ornate as if a great festival were on, and above all this the gleaming minaret of the Giralda is uplifted. And this narrow, crooked lane is called Sierpes because it twists like a snake ; here the life of Seville flows along densely and slowly : casinos and taverns, shops full of lace and flowered silk, caballeros in light Andalusian sombreros, tiny streets where vehicles cannot be driven, because of the crowds of people drinking wine, chatting, haggling, laughing and generally idling there in various ways. Then there is an old cathedral embedded in the old quarter among the houses and patios, so that you can only see bits of it wherever you are, as if it were too big to be viewed as a whole by mortal eye. And then another small faience church, miniature palaces with bright and graceful frontages, arcades and balconies and embossed lattices, a notched wall, from behind which palms and broad-leaved musas lean over ; always something attractive, a snug corner where you feel at ease and which you never want to forget. Just recall that wooden cross on the little square, as white and restful as a nun's cell ; those delightful, quiet

quarters of the city which contain the narrowest
streets and the most charming nooks in the
world——

Yes, it was there, twilight had fallen, and the
children in the street were dancing the *sevillana*
to the strains of an angelic barrel-organ ; somewhere thereabouts is Murillo's house—ye gods,
if I lived there, everything I wrote would be
tender and cheerful ; and there too, is the most
beautiful spot in the world ; it is called Plaza de
Doña Elvira or Plaza de Santa Cruz—no, these
are two spots, and now I do not know which is
the more beautiful, nor am I ashamed yet that I
was moved to tears by their beauty and my weari-
ness. Yellow and red frontages and a neat green
garden in the middle : a garden containing specimens of faience, box-trees, children and oleander,
an embossed crucifix and the evening peal of
bells ; and I, unworthy mortal in the midst of it
all, murmuring to myself in dazed accents : Good
Lord, why, this is like a dream or a fairy tale !

And then there is nothing more to be said, and
all that you can do is to surrender yourself to the
dazzling loveliness. Of course, you too ought to
be young and handsome ; you ought to have a
magnificent voice and be madly in love with a
beautiful maiden in a mantilla, and that will do.
Beauty is sufficient unto itself. But there are
various kinds of beauty ; among them the Sevillan
comeliness is particularly voluptuous and winsome, cosy and affectionate ; it has feminine

lushness with a crucifix on its bosom, it is fragrant with myrtle and tobacco, and takes its ease in seemly and sensual comfort. You seem to be, not in streets and squares, but in the passages and patios of a house where contented people dwell;

you walk along almost on tip-toe, but nobody asks you: what are you doing here, *caballero indiscreto*?

(There is also a large, brown, diapered Baroque palace; at first I thought it was a royal castle, but it turned out to be a government tobacco factory, the very one in which Carmen rolled cigarettes. A large number of these Carmens are still employed there, wearing an oleander blossom behind their ears and living at Triana, while Don José has become a gendarme in a three-cornered hat ; and Spanish cigarettes are still appallingly strong and black, no doubt through the influence of those dark girls from Triana.)

Rejas y Patios

JUST as the streets of Seville look like passages and courtyards, the windows of the apartments look like bird-cages hanging on the walls. You must know that they are all provided with a lattice and they project beyond the houses : these lattices are called *rejas*, and sometimes they are such beautiful specimens of metal-work in spirals, palmetas and wands, with all kinds of twisted and criss-cross patterns, that the proper thing to do would certainly be to sing a serenade beneath them about *sus ojitos negros* or *mi triste corazón* (m-brum brum, m-brum-brum, with guitar accompaniment). *Oiga, niña :*

> *Para cantarte mis penas*
> *hago hablar a mi guitarra*
> *si no entiedes lo que dice-e*
> *no digas que tienes alma* (m-brum)

For you have no idea how it adds to the attractiveness of a *niña* like that, when she is behind a lattice like a rare bird.

Altogether it would appear that embossed lattices form a speciality of national Spanish art ; never could I produce any verbal embossings and twirlings to match a church lattice, while as for

secular lattices, instead of a doorway there is a
fine lattice leading into every house, the windows
twinkle with lattices, and tendrils of flowers hang
from latticed balconies ; for which reason Sevilla
as a whole looks like a harem, like a cage, or—no,

La reja

wait a bit—it looks as if across it were stretched
chords, upon which your eyes strum an amorous
refrain to your enchantment. A Sevillan lattice
is not a lattice which encloses, but one which
forms a frame ; it is a decorative framework
affording a glimpse of the house. Ah, my friends,
those delightful glimpses of Sevillan patios, of

white anterooms inlaid with faience, of an open courtyard bestrewn with flowers and palms, of a tiny paradise where human families dwell!

House after house wafts upon you the shadowy coolness of its patio; and however poor it may be, the brick paving there is arrayed with a tiny

green jungle of flower-pots containing an aspidistra or two, oleander, myrtle and speedwell, and oozy dracaena and some sort of cheap and heavenly asparagus ; and not only that, but from the walls

are suspended flower-pots with tradescantia, syringa and cordyline, and panicum, and birdcages, while in the yard an old mammy takes her ease in a wicker-chair ; but there are also patios bordered with arcades and paved with majolica,

69

where a faience fountain gurgles, and latania and chamaerops spread their fans, and musa and coco-nut and kentia and phœnix arch their long leaves from a dense foliage of philodendra, aralia, clivia and yukka and evonymus, to say nothing of ferns, mesembrianthema, begonias and camelias and all the other curly, feathery, spiky and bulky forms of leafage in paradise lost. And all this is arranged in flower-pots in a tiny yard, and every house gives you the surprising impression of a palace when you peep through the shapely lattice into its patio which recalls paradise and denotes home.

Home and family. In every part of the world there are houses and dwellings, but there are two regions in Europe where the people have set up homes in the really full, traditional and poetical sense of the word. One is old-time England, overgrown with ivy, a place of fireside, arm-chairs and books ; and the other is Spain with the charming latticed glimpse of woman's realm, family life, the blossoming heart of the house. This lush, sweltering land has no family fireside ; it has the family patio where you can see the good people's homely comfort, their children, their daily festival. And I wager that it is a good thing to be a woman here, for she is crowned with the great glory and high honour of the household patio, amid a splendour of palms, laurels and myrtle. I believe that the beauty of the home is the special and potent glorification of woman ; it declares her rule, exalts her renown and surrounds her throne.   And by woman, I do not mean you, big-eyed muchacha, but your mama, the old, bearded lady in the wicker-chair —it is in her honour that I write this.

Giralda

THE Giralda is *the* landmark of Seville ; it is
so high that it is visible from every direction.
If in the course of your globe-trotting you per-
ceive, high above the house-tops, the gallery and
turret of the Giralda, why, you can be certain that
you are in Seville, for which you may thank your
lucky stars. Now the Giralda is a Moorish
minaret with Christian bells ; it is begirt with all
the beautiful devices of Arab decoration, and
right on the top of it there is a statue of Faith,
while the lower part is constructed of Roman and
Visigoth ashlars. That is just like Spain as a
whole ; it has Roman foundations, Moorish pomp
and a Catholic mind. Here Rome left only a
little of its urban civilization, but bequeathed
something more permanent—the Latin farmer,
which implies the Latin language. And this
provincial Latin rusticity was assailed by the
highly developed, luxurious, almost decadent
culture of the Moors. In its way it was a para-
doxical culture ; even in the highest stage of its
refinement it retained a nomadic imprint. Where
the Moors built castles and palaces you will
detect signs that they were originally tent-
dwellers. The Moorish patio is a cosy repre-

sentation of an oasis ; the gurgling fountain in
the Spanish courtyard, to this very day still
gratifies the desert dream of cool springs ; the

garden, represented by the contents of the flower-
pots, is a portable garden. The tent-dweller
packs up his home and all his luxuries so that he
can load them on asses ; that is why his home is

made of textiles and his luxuries are of filigree. His tent is his castle ; it is garnished with every pomp and splendour, but it is a pomp which a man can carry on his back ; it is woven and embroidered and stitched with goat's or lamb's wool ; and Moorish architecture has retained the delicate beauty and surface appeal of a woven fabric. The Moor even built lace-work archways and embroidered ceilings and walls interwoven with ornaments. And even though he could not pack up the Giralda and carry it away on mules, he bedecked its walls with a carpet pattern and a delicate fabric as if he had woven and sewn it while sitting on crossed legs. And when subsequently the Latin farmer and the Visigothic knight with sword and crucifix drove out the oriental sorcerer, they never got rid of this richly woven dream ; the Gothic *estilo florido*, the Renaissance *estilo plateresco*, the Baroque *estilo churrigueresco* are nothing but architectural diaper and embroidery and filigree quilting and lace-work, which covers and, dream-like, conceals the stone walls and transforms them into magical glistening draperies. The nation perished but its culture lives. This most Catholic of countries has never ceased to be Moorish. All this and many other things you could see with your own eyes on the Giralda of Seville.

And from the Giralda you can see the whole of Seville, so white and shiny that it makes your eyes ache, and pink with its flat, tiled house-tops

braided with faience cupolas and belfries and
battlements, palm-trees and cypresses ; and right
below, the huge, almost monstrous roof of the

cathedral, an eruption of pillars, Gothic turrets,
buttresses, groins and campaniles, and all around,
farther than the eye can see, the green and gold

plain of Andalusia, a-sparkle with glistening homes. But if your sight is good, you will see even more ; you will see families at the back of the patios, gardens on balconies and terraces and flat house-tops, wherever there is room for the smallest flower-pot, and women watering flowers or whitewashing their blanched cube of a house with a nice creamy coating of lime ; as if in this life there were nothing else to think of but beauty.

La Catedral

And now that we have the white town before us, let us make a pilgrimage to two places, which are particularly worthy of respect, and which are adorned with a whole set of masterly and worshipful works. The first is the cathedral. Every proper cathedral has two functions. To begin with, it is so big that it is entirely cut off from human habitations ; it stands in their midst like a sacred elephant among a herd of sheep, isolated and alien, a divine eminence projecting from the human ruck. And in the second place, as soon as you enter it, you find one huge open space amid the entrails of the town, larger in area than a market-place, larger than a city square ; when you arrive there from narrow lanes, yards and household dwelling-rooms it is like reaching a mountain-peak ; these pillars and vaulted roofs do not enclose a space, but with an ample sweep they extend it, thrusting a broad and high outlet amid the rabble of a mediaeval town. Here, my soul, heave a sigh of relief ; in the name of God you can take a deep and soothing breath.

La Catedral

But at this point of time I cannot tell you every-thing that was inside. Alabaster altars and vast lattices and the tomb of Columbus. Murillo and wood carvings, gold and traceries, marble and Baroque and retables and pulpits and many other Catholic objects which I did not even see ; for I looked at what surmounted it all, the five large, steep naves, quite a divine naval display, a sub-lime fleet swimming above the lustre of Seville ; in spite of all the art and all the culture amassed within its flanks, it contains an abundance of free and sacred space.

The other spot is the *ayuntamiento* or town hall. The exterior of Seville town hall is fairly plastered with relief and cornices, festoons and medallions and garlands, pilasters, caryatides, scutcheons and masks ; and inside, from ceiling to floor it is bestrewn with wood-carvings and canopies, gildings, faience, stucco and every variety of trappings such as the masters of every guild could devise. It is ostentiously done, and suggests that the city fathers were almost naive in their eagerness to show off ; it somehow recalls the good-natured dignity of the king of hearts or diamonds. These old town halls always move me by the emphasis with which they declare the renown and brilliance of the municipality ; I cannot help feeling that in them an ancient urban democracy established its throne and adorned it like an altar or like a royal residence.

Now when present-day democracy can afford a palace, it is a bank or a commercial building. In less progressive times it used to be a minster or a town hall.

Alcazar

FROM the outside it is a mediaeval, notched wall of bare ashlars; but within, it is a Moorish castle covered with verses from the Koran and bedecked from top to bottom with all the weird hocus-pocus and sorcery of the Orient. You must know that this Arabian Nights castle was built by Moorish architects for a Christian king. It was in the year of grace 1248 (as they say in the historical novels) when the Christian king Ferdinand entered the captured Moorish city of Seville on St. Clement's Day; but he was assisted in performing this Christian deed by one Ibn al Ahmar, Sultan of Granada, from which it is obvious that religion has always been hand in hand with politics. Whereupon the Christian king, for reasons which were doubtless pious and enlightened, drove three hundred thousand accursed Musulmans out of Seville; but three hundred years later the Moorish masters were building palaces for the Christian kings and hidalgos, and were covering their walls with subtle ornamentation and Cufic suras from the Koran. Which fact throws a peculiar twilight on the age-long struggle between Christians and Moors.

And if I had to describe the patios, the halls and the apartments of the Alcazar, I would set

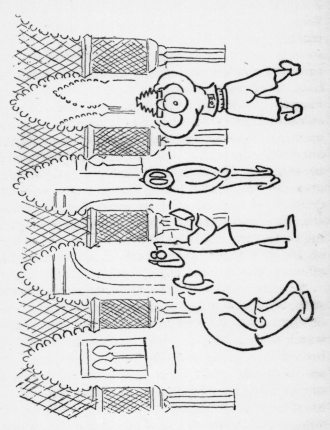

about the task like a builder; I would first of all collect the material, such as stone and majolica, stucco, marble and precious timbers, and whole

cartloads of the loveliest words for mixing the
mortar of my prose style ; then, as builders do,
I would start from the bottom, from the faience
floors ; on top of that I would place the slender
marble pillars, keeping a sharp eye on their
sockets and capitals, but I would pay particular
care to the walls inlaid with the choicest majolica
tiles, overspread with lacework of stucco, em-
blazoned with a whole delicate and lustrous
colour-scheme, pierced by windows, arcades,
apertures, trellises, *ajimez*, and galleries in accordance with the noble order of the horse-shoe, the
broken arch, the circle and the lobe ; whereupon,
above all this I would arch aloft the vaultings and
ceilings of stalactites, meshes and networks of
stucco, star-patterns, coffers, faiences, gold, tint-
ings and carvings, and having done all this, I
should feel thoroughly ashamed of my bungling
efforts ; for it cannot be described like that.

A better way would be for you to take a kaleido-
scope and turn it round and round until the sight
of that endless geometry makes you feel dizzy ;
watch the rippling of water until your senses are
benumbed ; drug yourself with hashish until you
see the whole world turning into an endless series
of dissolving patterns ; add to this everything that
intoxicates and beguiles, that is opalescent and
voluptuous ; everything that clouds the senses ;
everything that resembles lace and brocade, filigree and jewels, the treasure of Ali Baba, precious
fabrics, a stalactite dome and the mere stuff of

dream ; and through this many-tinted, fantastic and almost crazy array you must suddenly pass

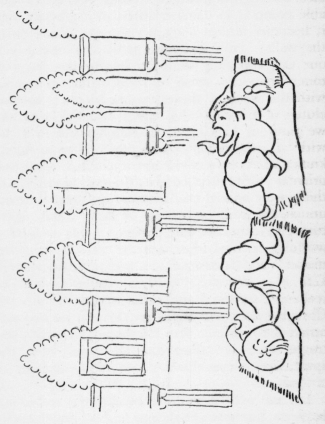

a comb so as to produce a tremendously neat, dainty and yet strict arrangement, a quiet and contemplative constraint, a sort of dreamy and

wise renunciation, which deploys these fairy-tale
treasures in an almost unmaterial and unreal surface, soaring upon fragile arcades. This unutter-
able pomp is so dematerialized in its surface that
it becomes almost a mere vision projected on to
the walls. How material, gross and ungainly is
our art, appealing almost more to the sense of
touch than the sense of sight, when compared
with the work of these strange Moors ; we just
clutch and handle the things which please us ;
we pass our hands over it roughly and brutally,
with a gesture of ownership. Heaven alone
knows what sense of the untrammelled, what vast
oriental spirituality led the Moorish architects to
this purely optical enchantment, to these dreamy,
unmaterial edifices, woven of lace, sheen, apertures, and kaleidoscopic patterns ; this altogether
worldly, sensual, luscious art actually quelled
matter and transformed it into a magical veil.
Life is a dream. On these terms it will be
realized that the Latin peasant and the Roman
Christian had to sweep away this too refined and
ornamental race. The European material and
tragic sense of values had to prevail over the
spiritualized sensualism of one of the noblest of
civilizations.

Let me add that, quite briefly, the difference
between European buildings and Moorish architecture is implicit in the fact that Gothic and,
indeed, Baroque, are built for spectators, standing
or kneeling, while Moorish architecture was

clearly intended for spiritual voluptuaries who, while lying on their backs, revelled in these magical arches, ceilings, friezes and endless decorative arabesques which were vaulted above their heads to provide them with the inexhaustible means for dreamy contemplation.

And all of a sudden these fantastic, delicate patios, enclosed within the notched wall, are invaded by a flock of white pigeons ; at this you realize, almost with amazement, the true meaning of this magical tectonic order ; it is absolute lyricism.

Jardines

THE gardens of the Alcazar, in their own particular way, are typical of Spanish gardens as a whole ; they contain, it is true, a few odds and ends which are to be seen nowhere else, such as, the baños or vaulted bath-room of Doña María de Padilla, the mistress of the Christian king Pedro the Cruel. It is said that, in accordance with the etiquette of the time, the caballeros of the court used to drink water from her bath ; but I don't believe this, because I have seen precious few caballeros in Seville drink water.

Now I have tried to describe from memory what a Spanish garden looks like ; but as there wasn't room for it on one sheet of paper, I had to make a threefold description :

1. A Spanish garden consists, first and foremost, of cypresses, clipped box-trees, myrtle, privet, laurel, holly, laurocerasas, honeysuckle, and suchlike diversely shaped shrubs, pyramids and spheres, from which by a process of clipping, linking and moulding are produced alleys and passages, vaults and arches, green ramparts, palings and borders, hedges, partitions and labyrinths, and, in fact, the whole ingenious geo-

metrical architecture of the old, severe school of gardening ; and in this sunny land it will be readily understood that this is not really a garden which produces plants, but a garden which produces shade.

2. In the second place the Spanish garden consists, first and foremost, of flagstones, bricks and glazed tiles, majolica flights of steps, faience

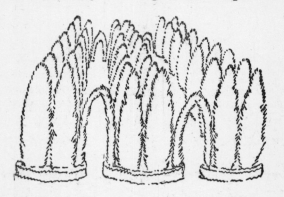

palings, roundels and seats ; further, of majolica tanks, fountains, cisterns, cascades, jets and runnels gurgling with a delicate trickle of water ; of faience pavilions, balconies, pergolas and balustrades ; wherein the aforesaid majolica is decorated with the neatest of black-and-white chequering, meshing, streaking, patterning or painting in ochre, indigo and Venetian scarlet ; and this faience world teems with flower-pots : flower-pots containing camelias, fig-plants, azaleas, abutilons, begonias and coleuses, chrysanthemums and asters ; whole avenues and clusters of flower-pots baked to a turn ; flower-pots on the ground,

on the rims of shallow water-troughs, on terraces and on steps.

3. In the third place, the Spanish garden con-

sists, first and foremost, of a most luxuriant jungle, of a tropical brushwood thrusting forth a regular jet of palms, cedars and plane-trees, entwined with bougainvillæa, clematis, aristolochiæ, begonia, as well as large-leaved shoots with flowers resembling the convolvulus, which plant is known here as " campanilla," also other shoots blossoming like thorn-apple, which, too, is called " campanilla," and other creeping plants, blossoming like a huge clematis and likewise named " campanilla " ; then there are dracæna and date-palms, chamærops, acacias, phœnix-palms, and —how on earth am I to know all their names ? If you only knew the kind of leaves they have ! Glossy and stringy, tufted like ostrich feathers, unsheathed like broad-swords, fluttering like banners ; and you can take my word for it, that if Eve clad herself in one of these leaves, it was not to cover her shame, but for the sake of display and luxury. In this dense paradisical forest there is no room for the tender bud or the blade of grass ; it may be that they cultivate grass here only in flower-pots.

I have described this trio for you in three separate sketches ; but in reality the whole thing grows in one single spot, which of course, baffles description. The Spanish garden represents, at the same time, a clipped system of gardening, crammed with miniature faience fountains, terraces, roundels and steps, littered with flower-pots, draped with palm-jungles and creepers ;

and the whole lot sometimes occupies no more than a bare handful of ground studded with fountains and runnels ; never have I seen gardens so amazingly concentrated and intensified as in Spain. An English park is a cultivated land-

scape ; a Spanish garden is an artificial paradise. A French park is a monumental edifice ; a Spanish garden is an intimate dream. In those nooks soft with shade, gurgling waters, cool majolica, dazing fragrance and tropical leafage is the gentle tread of another, a more pleasure-loving race ; here, too, the Moors have left their traces.

Mantillas

ALL that follows is intended in honour and praise of the ladies of Seville. They are petite and dark, dark-haired, with dark frisky eyes, and mostly in dark attire ; they have tiny hands and feet, as required by the old lyrics of chivalry,  and they look as if they were just on their way to confession, that is, they are saintly and rather sinful in appearance. But what gives them particular splendour and dignity is the *peineta*, the lofty tortoise-shell comb, with which every lady of Seville is crowned ; a sumptuous and triumphal comb, like a crown or a halo. This ingenious superstructure transforms every dark chiquita into a tall, grand lady ; with a thing like that on her head she just has to walk proudly, to carry her head like a sacrament and to let only her eyes dart about, which accordingly the ladies of Seville do.

The second and even greater glory of the ladies
of Seville is the mantilla, a lace wrap flung across
the queenly comb ; the mantilla, which is black

or white, like the veil of the Moslem women, the
cowl of the penitent, the mitre of the pontiff and
the helmet of the conqueror ; the mantilla, which

serves to crown woman and, at the same time, to conceal her and make her shimmer more alluringly. Never have I seen women wearing anything more dignified and subtle than this garb which blends nunnery, harem and the veil of the beloved.

But allow me to stop and extol these women

of Seville. What self-assurance, what national pride these dark chulas must have to make them prefer the ceremonious and antique *peineta* and mantilla to all enticements of the world's fashions. Seville is by no means a village ; Seville is a rich, vivacious city, the very air of which is amorous ; if the ladies of Seville keep to their mantillas, that is firstly because it suits them, and secondly because they set store by being Spanish beauties in all their antique renown ; but the chief thing is that it suits them.

If the ladies of Seville are not crowned, they are at least wreathed ; above their ears, in their black hair they carry a whole nosegay, or at least a rose, a camelia or an oleander-blossom ; and across their shoulders and arms they wear a silk

shawl, with an embroidery of large roses, heavy tassels and a knot at the bosom ; or a mantón de Manilla, which is a silk mantle, shawl or robe,

studded with an embroidery of roses and tassels,
but it has to be worn with an air. It is flung in
a series of folds across arms and shoulder, then
it is drawn together tightly, the hands are placed
akimbo, the dainty croup is braced outward, and
below, there is a clatter of wooden heels ; I tell
you, to wear the mantón properly demands great
skill as a dancer.

What struck me was that Spanish women have
contrived to preserve two great feminine privi-
leges : servitude and homage. The Spanish
woman is guarded like a treasure, after curfew
you will not meet a girl in the streets, and I have
even seen street-walkers accompanied by dueñas,
evidently to protect their honour. I have heard
that every male member of a family, from the
remotest great-uncle down to the grandson, has
the right and the duty to watch, with sword in
hand, so to speak, over the maidenly honour of
his sisters, female cousins and other relatives.
No doubt there is just a little of the spirit of the
harem in this ; but at the same time it shows a
great respect for the particular dignity of woman.
While man prides himself on his worth as a
cavalier and protector, to woman is vouchsafed
the renown and prestige of a guarded treasure ;
whereby both sides, as far as honour is concerned,
get their fair share.

But, really, what pleasant folk they are : youths
in Andalusian broad-brimmed hats, ladies in
mantillas, girls with a nosegay behind their ears

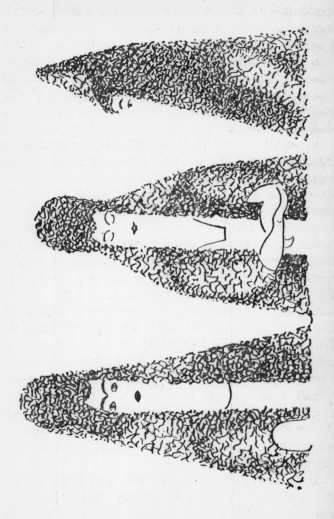

and dark optics beneath drooping eyelids ; it is good to see how light-footedly they bear themselves, with the strutting gait of pigeons, how they flirt, and with what passion and seemliness their eternal wooings are fraught ! And life itself here is sonorous, yet without any uproar ; in the whole of Spain I did not hear a single quarrel or a cross word, possibly because a quarrel would mean the use of a knife ; don't take it amiss if I refrain from telling you which of these two methods shows a higher sense of decorum.

Triana

TRIANA is the gipsy and working-class quarter of Seville on the other side of the Guadalquivir ; besides this, Triana is a special kind of dance, as well as a ditty of its own kind, just as Granadinas are typical songs of Granada,

Murcianas of Murcia, Cartageneras of Cartagena and Malaguenas of Malaga. Just imagine Brixton having its own sort of dance and Golders Green its national poetry ; or Birmingham having an entirely different musical folk-lore from Ipswich, and Winchester, let us say, being distinguished

by a particularly passionate and eccentric dance.
I am not aware that Winchester has gone to such
lengths yet.

Of course, I trotted off to have a look at the
gipsies of Triana ; it was Sunday evening, and
I expected to find Gitanas
dancing there at every
street-corner to the sound
of the tambourine ; I
expected too that they
would drag me off to their
camp and that terrible
things would befall me ;
still, I resigned myself to
my fate, and off I went
to Triana. Nothing what-
ever happened ; not that
there was any lack of
gipsies, male and female,
there ; the place swarms
with them, but there is
no camp. There are only
some tiny cottages with
clean patios, with a regular
gipsyish abundance of
children, mothers suckling
their babies, almond-eyed girls with a red flower
in their blue-black hair, slender gipsy-lads with
a rose between their teeth, a peaceable Sunday
crowd taking its ease on its doorsteps. I, too,
took my ease among them and hurled almond-

eyed glances at the girls there. I can testify that most of them are of pure, handsome Indian type, with their eyes just a trifle aslant, with olive-coloured skin and fine teeth ; moreover, the movement of their croup is even more supple than that of the girls in Seville. That must be enough for you ; it was enough for me in that melting night at Triana.

And because I was satisfied with little, the local deity of Triana rewarded me with a full-blown romería. Suddenly, in the distance a clatter of castanets became audible, and through the narrow street of Triana glided a high car, dragged by oxen and festooned with wreaths and an abundance of tulle curtains, canopies, trimmings, flounces, drapery, veils and all sorts of other fallals, and the nice white body of the car was full up inside with girls who were clicking the castañuelas and singing at the top of their voices, as people do sing in Spain. I solemnly assure you that this garnished car, illuminated with a red fancy lantern, had the strange voluptuous aspect of a marriage-bed filled with girls. Each one in turn obliged with a loud seguidilla, while the rest kept time with their clattering castanets, clapped their hands and made shrill noises. And round the next corner a similar car was gliding along with a load of bedizened, shouting and clattering girls. And then there was a carriage drawn by a team of five donkeys and mules, driven by caballeros in Andalusian sombreros. And there were other caballeros on prancing horses. I asked the by-standers what this meant, and they said that it was the *vuelta de la romería*, *¿ sabe ?* I must explain that a romería is a pilgrimage to some

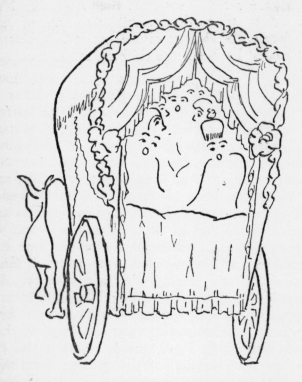

sacred spot in the vicinity, to which the populace of Seville, especially the populace of both sexes, goes on foot and in conveyances ; and on the girls' petticoats there are broad flounces or whatever they're called, and they cackle like a cartload of sparrows.

And when, amid the clatter of castanets, the merry romería had disappeared in the street of Triana, the regional secret of the castañuelas was revealed to me : they recall the song of the nightingale, the chirrup of crickets and the clatter of donkeys' hoofs on the cobbles, all in one.

Corrida

BY chance, while I am writing this, the cat has climbed on to my lap and is purring away for all she is worth. Now I must admit that, although the animal is really in my way and won't take no for an answer, I somehow couldn't bring it over myself to kill her with a spear or an espada, whether on foot or on horseback. So you mustn't think that I'm a bloodthirsty or brutal person, although I witnessed the defeat of six bulls, and didn't go away until it was the turn of the seventh one, and even then not on moral grounds, but rather because it had begun to bore me. For one thing, the corrida was dull ; my opinion is that those bulls were too tough.

I may say that during the bull-fights I had very mixed feelings ; there were amazing moments which I shall never forget, and painful junctures when I wished that the earth would swallow me up. The finest sight of all is, of course, the solemn entry of the toreadors into the arena ; what you ought to see is the yellow sand beneath the blue sky, the circular plaza de toros, packed with people ; on top of that the trumpets begin to blare, and the embroidered alguacilillos ride into the arena ; after them, in showy jackets and gold-bespangled cloaks, cocked hats and silk knickers, the matadores, espadas, banderilleros and picadores on their mares and the chulos and the teams of mules, four-in-hand, festooned with bells ; and they all bear themselves so grandly and yet so buoyantly that no opera chorus on earth can hold a candle to them.

But that day there was something special on the programme : a " frente a frente " contest,

i.e. a forehead-to-forehead struggle between two matador soloists, who keep up the old tradition of the aristocratic corrida on horseback. One was Don Antonio Cañero, a riding-master from Cordoba, who was dressed in Andalusian style, and the other was Joao Branco Nuncio, a Portuguese rejoneador in blue rococo attire. First of all Don Antonio pranced into the arena on an Andalusian stallion, saluted the Infanta and the President as a cavalier should, and then, with horse and sombrero, brandished a salute to everybody ; next, the gate flew open, and in dashed a black bundle of muscles, a bull with a chest and neck like a crag, stopped short, dazzled by the hot glare of the sun, lashed his tail, and in a cheerful sort of way darted after an enemy who, holding a thin lance, was waiting for him on horseback in the middle of the arena. I should like to describe what followed, step by step ; but where am I to get the words

from, which would do justice to this dance of the bull, the horse and the rider ? A fighting bull is a fine sight when he stands there panting, as glossy as asphalt, a volcanic animal who until then has been provoked to the pitch of frenzy by being kept in a cage ; now he was standing still, his hoofs wedged in the ground, and with flaming eyes he searched for the opponent whom he should overwhelm. And then the horse pranced up to him with graceful, ceremonious movements, waggling its flanks like a ballet-dancer and lifting itself on its sinews ; the pitch-black heap of muscularity began to ripple, and dashed forth in a terrific onslaught, his horns nearly touching the ground, with the momentum of a projectile and the unexpected elasticity of a chunk of indiarubber. I must confess that at that moment the palms of my hands went damp with fear, just as once before when I was climbing a mountain and my foot slipped. It was only just a moment ; two leaps, and the prancing horse, at a seemly gallop, lifting its feet high, was wheeling behind the bull's bony rump. The cheering which burst forth like a volley, checked the indiarubber tank in his headstrong dash ; it seemed to have annoyed the bull ; he swished his tail and dashed off at a gallop after the horse. But the bull's tactics are to attack point-blank ; the tactics of the horse and rider are to wheel in circles. The bull, with his horns well forward, rushed along with the intention of seizing and tossing his enemy with a terrific blow ; suddenly he came to a standstill with an air of amazement and looking rather stupid, when he found that he was faced with nothing but the empty arena. But his tactics are not only to gore but also to maul with a dreadful slantwise wrench ; even his impetuous onslaught is sometimes delayed by a sudden side movement, straight towards the horse's weak spots ; I really can't tell you whether it was the horse or the rider who first realized that this tricky move was coming, but I shouted and clapped with enormous relief when at the very next instant the splendid horse was performing his pirouettes five yards further on. I rather fancy that the horse, too, puts all his heart and nerve into this jousting, because every five minutes the rejoneador gallops off behind the barrier and comes back on a fresh horse.

Now this dance is so gorgeous and exciting that I almost forgot to mention that those who take part in it are out to kill; or rather, I forgot it while I was still actually in the arena. I had noticed, of course, that more than once during an onrush the rejoneador propped himself up with his lance against the bull's neck, but the bull merely shook himself and galloped on ; it looked as if they were just playing. The second lance lodged in his neck and stuck there quivering, just like a penholder when the point of the nib has got fixed in the floor. The bull tried desperately to shake away the thing that had bitten its way into his throat ; he jerked his head to and fro, he stood up on his hind-legs ; but the spike was firmly fixed in that solid mass of muscle. There stood the bull, scooping the sand with his feet, as if he wanted to dig himself in, and he bellowed with pain and anger ; froth trickled from his jowl—perhaps that is how a bull sheds tears. But now the horse with his opponent was able to

raise itself briskly and nimbly in front of him.
The wounded bull stopped roaring, began to
snort, humped his back and made a frenzied onslaught. I closed my eyes, because I expected
that this would lead to a tangle of crushed and
mauled legs and bodies in the sand of the arena.
When I opened my eyes, the bull stood there with

his head upraised ; the broken lance was twitching
to and fro in his neck, while the horse was tripping
along towards him like a ballet-girl ; only its
drooping ears showed any sign of terror. What
a stout heart this colt has ; what daring, what
elegance in the aspect of this smart rider who
manages his horse with his knees, while he plunges
his eyes into those of the bull ; but what a magnificent and natural hero is this bull which, though
he can weep, cannot retreat. The man masters

the horse, and ambition masters the man ; but all
the bull wants is to be alone in the arena : who is
putting himself between me and all the cows in
the world ? See, now he is lowering his forehead,
and once more he dashes forward full-tilt, with
all his terrific bulk against this one opponent who
trips along the arena ; he hurls himself like a
rock, but there are moments when the sinews of
his feet suddenly give way in a ghastly manner.
Is he wavering ? No, that is nothing ; full speed
ahead ! Three cheers for the bull ! At this
moment the third lance shot out like lightning.
The bull staggered and then pulled himself
together ; he was just about to brace his muscles
for a new clash, when suddenly he lay down almost
peacefully like a cow chewing the cud. The rider
drove his horse round the resting warrior. Now
the bull made a lunge as if he were about to jump
up, but then he seemed to change his mind : well,
perhaps, after all, I'll rest here a little. At this
the rider wheeled round on his horse and galloped
from the arena amid a drum-fire of clapping and
shouting. The bull laid his head on the ground as if
resting only a moment, only an instant, whereupon
his body relaxed and braced itself again, his legs
gawkily stretched themselves out, and queerly,
almost unnaturally projected from the black bulk
of his body. Rigor mortis. From the opposite
gate, a team of mules comes rushing in, with a
tinkle of bells ; after a few seconds, amid a
flicking of whips, they drag the burden of the

dead bull at a gallop through the sand of the arena.

Well, I have kept nothing from you as to how it strikes a spectator. Is it magnificent or cruel ? I do not know ; what I saw was, if anything, most magnificent ; and when I look back at it now—

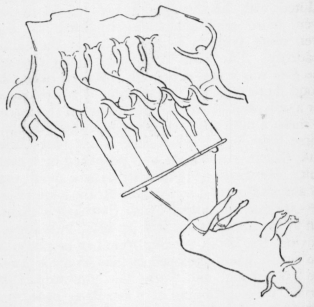

I cannot help wondering whether it would be better for that dauntless and noble specimen of a bull to end in the shambles by being banged on the head with a bludgeon ! Would that be more humane than for him to perish this way in a fight, as befits his mettlesome and pugnacious heart ?

Well, I don't know ; but it was a relief to me when I was able to look at the empty arena, yellow as fire, beneath the blue sky and surrounded by a noisy and excited crowd.

Now the blue, showy Portuguese cantered into the circle, galloped round the arena, turned and saluted with his headgear ; his mount moved even more trippingly, and it lifted its legs even more prettily, as prescribed by the riding academy. The black bull which burst through the gate was a bad-tempered, stubborn beast ; he stood there hunched up, with his horns prepared for a sally, but he would not let himself be enticed to make a dash ; it was only when the trembling horse trippingly marked time a few paces from him, that he rushed out as if propelled by a catapult. He was so sure of what he was about, that he almost turned a somersault on the spot where he expected the impact with the horse's chest ; but at the same instant that his black bulk started moving, the horse, turning round in response to the rider's knees, galloped off like an arrow from the bow-string, and fairly flew onwards, then turned while galloping at a headlong pace, and trotted back in gavotte time to the snorting bull. Never have I seen a rider so perfectly blended with his horse ; a rider who sat motionless in the saddle whether galloping or jumping, who could turn his horse in the fraction of a second, pull him up short, make him rear, get him, while at the gallop, to tackle a high jump, a long jump and other capers which I do not even know the names of; and all the time he held the reins lightly in one hand as if they were a cobweb, while in the other lurked the murderous barb of the lance. But now just bear in mind that this feat of horsemanship was performed by a rococo dandy, face to face with the horns of an infuriated bull—it is true that in this particular instance the sharp tops of the horns were made safer by means of rubber nobs; bear in mind, I say, that he slipped away, jumped aside and attacked, darted off like an arrow and bounded back like a piece of india-rubber, grazed the bull with his spear while racing along at full speed, broke the shaft of his lance, and then defenceless, with the fuming beast full tilt after him, cantered to the barrier for a new lance. At the gallop he thrust three spears home, and then, taking no further notice of the bull, pranced out of the arena; the bellowing animal still had to be attended to with a sword, and, to wind up with, the puntillero had to run a dagger through him. It was a revolting piece of butchery.

The third bull was dealt with by two competitors. The Portuguese had the first spear; while he was dallying in front of the bull's uncovered horns, the Andalusian was marking time on his colt, ready to join the fray at a moment's notice. But the third bull meant business; truculent and astoundingly quick, he did not stop attacking from the moment when, amid clouds of

dust and sand, he dashed into the arena. Lunge followed lunge ; this bull was quicker than the horse, and chased the rider all over the arena. But suddenly he took it into his head to have a go at the expectant Andalusian. The Andalusian turned his horse round and fled ; the bull stubbornly followed him and caught him up. This is the moment when the rejoneador, to protect himself and his horse, lets fly with his spear to stop the bull's little game ; but, in this case, the first spear belonged to the Portuguese. The Andalusian lowered his outstretched spear, then, with heaven alone knows what effort of strength, dragged the horse aside, and scurried away amid tremendous cheering and shouting ; for the Spaniards appreciate a feat like that. The Portuguese took charge of his bull and led it forward at a gallop ; while racing along he took aim with his lance, but the bull just jerked his head, and the spear flew a long way off into the sand. It was now the Spaniard's turn ; he took charge of the bull and tried to tire him out by letting himself be chased all over the arena. Meanwhile, Don Joao came back with a fresh horse, and looked on. This bull seemed to have a strategy of his own ; he hounded the Andalusian to the barrier, attacking his left flank. Suddenly the audience rose up in their excitement ; the bull had now caught up the rider on his uncovered left flank ; at this, the blue rococo dandy dashed out full tilt against the bull, the horse reared and jumped aside, the bull jerked his head towards his new opponent who now flinched back ; but at that instant the Andalusian had already twisted his horse round and thrust his lance into the bull's neck, like a knife into a lump of butter. Whereupon the crowd stood up and cheered ; and I, who never, not even in books, can find anything attractive about toying with death, for death is

neither a joke nor a spectacle—I had a lump in my throat ; of course, this was the result of horror, but of admiration as well. For the first time in my life I beheld chivalry, in accordance with the formula : with arms in hand, face to face with death, risking life for the honour of the thing. Reader, I cannot help myself : there *is* something in it ; something great and splendid. But not even the third spear finished off this astounding bull ; again a man had to come rushing up with a dagger—and the crowd swarmed over the arena, which lay there clean and yellow amid the blue Sevillan sabbath.

Lidia Ordinaria

THE second part of the corrida was a fight on ordinary lines, which is more dramatic, but also more distressing. I should not like to judge all bull-fights on the strength of that one, because it was an unlucky day. The very first bull, when the banderillas reached him, went mad and made a stubborn attack ; but the shouting crowd did not want him to get tired out at the very start ; so there was a blare of trumpets, the arena was emptied, and Palmeño, the gold-bespangled espada, went to pink the bull. But the animal was still too quick ; at the first onset he gored Palmeño in the groin, tossed him in a semicircle over his head, and dashed up to his powerless body. I had previously seen an infuriated bull tearing and trampling on a cloak which had been cast aside. It was a moment when my heart really missed a beat. At this particular instant a torero arrived on the scene with a cloak and hurled himself straight at the horns of the bull, whose eyes he covered with the mantilla ; he then made the attacking bull follow him. Meanwhile two chulos lifted up the hapless Palmeño and carried the handsome, unconscious fellow off at a canter. " Pronóstico reservado " was the report which the next day's papers published about his injuries.

Now if I had left immediately after this incident, I should have been haunted by the memory of one of the most impressive sights I have ever witnessed : a chulo, whose name was not even mentioned in the papers, exposed his stomach to the bull's horns, to get him away from the wounded

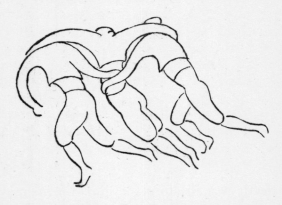

matador ; without hesitation he diverted the madly attacking bull towards himself, and at the last instant just managed to leap out of his way ; another torero had already arrived, and with a cloak was attracting the bull towards him, so that the first man could wipe the sweat from his forehead with a gilt-diapered sleeve. Then the two ornamented men withdrew, and a new espada, sword in hand, took the place of the crack performer who had been wounded.

The matador sobresaliente was a man with a long, dismal face, and was evidently no favourite. He proceeded to take charge of the bull, who was what might be called a bad hat. From this moment onward the corrida degenerated into a shocking display of butchery, when the frenzied crowd by their shouting and whistling fairly hurled the unpopular espada right at the horns of the savage animal ; and with clenched teeth,

as if death was in store for him, the man went too, and with an uncertain hand pinked the bull. The bull dragged away the sword which had got fixed in the wound, where it was jerking to and fro. A fresh shout of disapproval. The toreros ran up to keep the bull busy with their cloaks. The mob hounded them on with fierce shouts : it was eager for the bull to die a chivalrous death, come what may. The pale matador set out once again to slay with sword and cudgel, in accordance with the rules of the game ; but the bull then would not budge an inch, and stood still with upraised head, his neck bristling with banderillas, and garbed, so to speak, with a mantle of blood. The espada, with the point of his sword, made

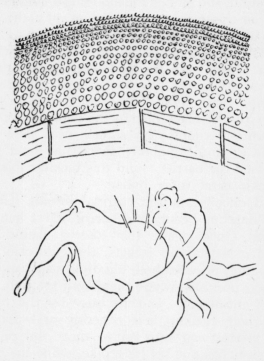

him lower his head so that he could pierce his shoulder, but the bull stood there mooing like a cow. The toreros flung cloaks over the banderillas embedded in his neck, thinking that the fresh pangs of pain would goad him out of his glum obstinacy ; but the pain made the bull bellow and pass water, and then he scraped his feet, as if he wanted to hide himself in the ground. At last the matador got him to lower his head to the ground, and pinked the motionless animal ; but not even this wound finished him off ; the puntillero also had to fling himself like a weasel upon the bull's neck, and ran him through with a dagger. Amid the frantic laughter and outcries of twenty thousand people the lanky matador, all glittering with gold, departed with a small, shaggy tuft of black hair in the nape of his neck, as tradition enjoins ; his sunken eyes were fixed on the ground. Nobody shook his hand when he passed the barrier ; and this luckless man had to tackle three more bulls.

And once again the corrida unfolds itself in all its dazzling beauty and horror, like a haunting dream. Once again the toreros flaunt their gilded mantlets and jackets, the gold-clad picadores enter on wretched, blindfold nags, and take up their positions where they await the bull, who, in the meanwhile, is kept busy by the toreros with their cloaks, their capering and dodging. The toreros egg him on to meet the picador, who stretches out his long pike, while his blindfold nag shivers with fright and would like to rear, if it could still manage such a feat. Now this particular bull was nothing loth, and with zest made a dash straight for the picador ; he bumped his neck against the lance, and it was a marvel that he did not fling the picador from the saddle ; but he only shook himself and started off again at a headlong gallop, caught the bony jade, rider and all, on his horns and hurled them on to the planks of the barrier. At the present day, by order of the dictator, the belly and chest of the picador's nag must be covered with a mattress, so that although the bull generally knocks it over and lays it out, he rarely rips its flank open, as used to happen ; all the same, the interlude with the picadors is brutal and stupid ; you know, it simply doesn't seem decent to watch that decrepit gelding convulsively struggling, or to drag it along to make it submit to the bull's terrific onslaught, then to set it on its legs again and hound it once more against the bull's horns ; for with the blunt spear these two picadors have to inflict three deep wounds on the bull, so that he may lose a little blood and be " castigado." The fight itself may be a fine spectacle ; but the terror, reader, the terror of beast and man alike, is an appalling and ignoble sight. And when horse, rider and spear are mingled in a regular welter, the toreros come leaping forward with their cloaks and take away the snorting bull, who always wins this first skirmish—at the cost of an ugly wound between the shoulder-blades.

Then the picadores trot off, the bull becomes infuriated by the red linings of the cloaks, and the banderillos come trotting into the arena.

They are, if anything, even more resplendent than the others, and in their hands they carry their javelins, or rather long wooden darts, decorated with paper frills and ribbons; they trip along in front of the bull, call him names, wave their arms and rush towards him to try

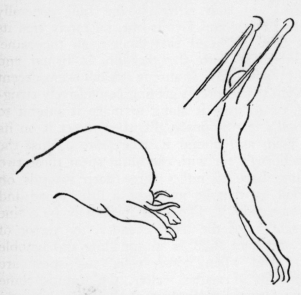

and induce him to make a blind, rampageous attack with lowered head and outstretched neck. At the instant when the bull rushes out, the banderillo raises himself on tiptoe, arches his back like a bow, and, taking aim with the banderillas in his hands raised on high, waits. I must say that there is something extremely fine about this easy, elegant posture of a man facing a raging beast. In the last fraction of the instant the two banderillas hurtle like lightning, the banderillero leaps aside and departs at a trot, while the bull jumps about in the queerest manner, trying to shake away the two darts which are waggling to and fro in his neck. After a while he gets another pair of beribboned banderillas fixed in him, and the nimble banderillero saves himself by jumping over the barrier. By this time the bull is bleeding profusely, his huge neck is drenched with regular honeycombs of blood ; with the banderillas sticking out of him he calls to mind the Heart of Our Lady of the Seven Sorrows.

And once again the chulos came running up to provoke and, at the same time, to tire the bull with their cloaks ; for the bull must not be allowed to get sluggish. They waved the red lining in front of him ; the bull blindly rushed out against the ample surface presented by the cloak, and the torero just managed by a single step to avoid the horns. But this bull tried to amuse the crowd ; he rushed against the toreros in such brisk and aggressive style that they all jumped over the barrier with the agility of fleas. At this the bull just lashed his tail, with one leap bounded over the barrier after them, and chased them into the narrow passage between barrier and public. The whole staff connected with the corrida scuttled away into the arena to save itself ; the bull triumphantly trotted through the

passage and returned to the arena, proudly swishing its tail ; and by making another rush it flung every living soul across the barrier. Now he was sole master of the arena and he showed that he realized it, too ; he seemed to be testily

urging the whole amphitheatre to applaud him. Once more the chulos came running out to tease him a little. The crowd gave vent to a roar ; it wanted to fling the espada on to the animal in all its magnificent strength. The gold-bespangled espada with the sunken eyes and lips pressed tightly together stood in front of the president's private box, a red muleta in his left hand and a drooping sword in his right ; he plainly did not care what happened ; he was waiting for the president to give a sign, but the president hesitated. The toreros was leaping round the bull who was chasing them away at the tips of his horns. The crowd rose up

threateningly and yelled. The waiting espada lowered his head with its black tuft of hair at the back and the president nodded ; thereupon trumpet-blasts resounded, the arena was emptied in a trice, and the espada with sword upraised, with motionless countenance was promising the bull his death. Then alone, brandishing his muleta, he entered the arena to cope with the bull.

This corrida was not a good one. The espada risked his life with a courage which was little short of desperate ; but the bull gave him no chance to score a hit, and chased him along over the sand, took his muleta away on his horns, and then harried the unprotected matador, who saved himself by getting across the barrier, but lost his sword in the process. At times this jousting of man and animal is superb ; the espada, with his muleta in front of him, tries to lure the animal on ; the bull makes a dash at the red rag, the man slips aside, and with his sunken eyes searches for a spot on the bull's neck where he can fix his weapon. All this is the work of an instant ; and then once again, an attack, a feint and a blow which misses its aim. This duel between bull and man is such a strain on the nerves that after a while you feel dazed. Several times the chulos ran out to relieve the espada, who was on his last legs, but with a yell the public drove them away ; thereupon the espada feebly shrugged his shoulders, and once more went for the bull. He squared up to him nicely, but his pinking was a failure. It was not until he was using his fifth sword that the bull succumbed ; it was an awful business ; when the espada left, he looked as if somebody had given him a sound thrashing, and the whole amphitheatre hissed him ; I felt more agonizingly sorry for him than for the bull who was breathing his last.

The sixth bull was a huge, white creature,

weak on his legs and with no more fight in him than a cow ; they almost had to push him along before he made an unsteady rush towards the picador's nag. The toreros with their cloaks drew him along by the horns to make him put up some sort of opposition ; and the banderilleros jumped about in front of him like mad, waving their arms, calling him names and jeering at him, to egg him on to what turned out to be a half-hearted and ungainly attack. The crowd whooped with resentment ; they wanted the bull to fight, and the result of this was that worse torture was inflicted on the blood-stained, bellowing animal. I wanted to leave ; but the people were standing up, shaking their fists and making a racket ; there was no chance of getting through, and so I covered my eyes and waited for it to stop. When, after what seemed an infinitely long time I opened my eyes, the bull was still alive, staggering about on shaky legs.

It was not until the seventh bull came on the scene that I managed to push my way out. As I rambled through the streets of Seville, I had a queer feeling of shame, but I really do not know whether my callousness or my weakness was the cause of it. There in the amphitheatre, at one particular moment, I had begun to protest that it was a brutal business ; next to me sat a Dutch engineer who had settled in Seville, and he was astonished at my protest. " This is my ninth corrida," he said to me, " but it was only the first one which seemed brutal." " This was a bad corrida," a Spaniard informed me by way of soothing my feelings ; " but you ought to see what a good one is like." Perhaps ; but it is hardly likely that I shall ever see a more heart-rending figure than that lanky, gaudily-dressed fellow with the face of an ox-herd and woebegone,

sunken eyes, whose shoulders were weighed down with the resentment of twenty thousand people. If I had known enough Spanish, I should have gone up to him and said : Juán, things will go wrong with us sometimes ; but bitter is the bread of man who depends upon the favour of the public.

And I reflect on this : in Spain I never actually saw the whip used on a horse or a mule ; the dogs and cats in the streets are trustful and affectionate, which shows that they are well treated. The Spaniards are not cruel to animals. The corrida is a struggle between man and beast which, in its essentials, is as old as time ; it has all the beauty of a struggle, but its pangs as well. Perhaps the Spaniards can view this beauty and this struggle in so perfect a light that they do not even see the cruelty which accompanies it. It certainly offers plenty to feast the eyes on, plenty of superb feats of agility, plenty of danger and magnificent courage—but another time I would keep away from a corrida.

And here the voice of temptation in my heart adds : unless a champion espada were there.

Flamencos

" FLAMENCO " means Flemish—but curiously enough there is nothing at all Flemish about the flamenco ; it suggests rather something gipsy-like and Moorish, a mixture of the orient and a night-club in equal parts. Nobody could explain to me why it is called flamenco, but the northern Spaniards rather object to it precisely because of its oriental flavour. A flamenco is singing and dancing and strumming on guitars, a clapping of hands and a clattering of castanets and wooden heels, and on top of all that there is shouting. And the Flamencos are singers, dancers, ballerinas and guitar-players, who from midnight onwards perform their tricks in nocturnal haunts. These popular songsters have such names as Cadiz Joe, Málaga Game-Leg, Valencia Snub-Nose or the Utrera Lad ; often they are gipsies and their fame extends beyond the frontiers of their province, according to their ability in sustaining trills. I really do not know how to set about explaining all this to you. Let's try it in alphabetical order :

Alza : ¡ Ole ! ¡ Joselito ! ¡ Bueno, bueno !

Bailar : Most of the Andalusian dances are solo

dances ; the guitars strum a jerky, tinkling
prelude, the seated troop begin to bestir
themselves, beat time with their feet, clap
their hands, begin to rattle the castanets ;
suddenly one of them rises, his arms fly up
in the air and his legs begin to perform a
frenzied dance with lots of stamping about
it. Take a Highland fling, a cake-walk, a

tango, a Cossack gopak, an Apache dance,
a fit of frenzy, unconcealed lechery and other
frantic movements, kindle them to a white
heat, and begin to batter them with castanets,
shouting all the while ; then the mixture
would begin to twirl as the flamenco dance
twirls, with impassioned pauses in melody
and dance amid a deafening rhythmic clatter
of the castanets. Unlike Northern dances,

the Spanish dance occupies not only the feet, but the whole swaying body and especially the arms which are flung upward with a snapping of the fingers against the castanets, while the feet perform dancing movements, which involve much stamping and beating of the heels on the ground. You might

almost say that the feet only provide an accompaniment to the dance, which occupies the flanks and arms, as well as the trunk braced in a curve and undulating amid the wild clatter of castanets and heels. The Spanish dance is a mysterious and, in effect, an orchestral interplay of the sharp, percussive rhythm of strings, castanets, tambourines and heels, with the supple flowing curve of the body as it dances. The music and all its appurtenances, including the shouting and clapping of hands, sets a whirling tempo which is boisterously increased or slackened like the beating of the heart ; but the body as it dances to the music plays a fluid solo violin melody, thrilling and passionate, a melody which exults, allures and laments, stormily swept along by the throbbing rhythm of the uproar accompanying the dance.

Brindar : Whereupon the guitars crash forth an ear-splitting note fit to break the strings in two, the onlookers begin to shout, and hand the dancer their glasses to drink a toast from.

Cantar : The cantos flamencos are sung in this way : the singer, whose name is Niño de Utrera or something of that sort, sits down on a chair among the guitar-players, who plunge into a jangling overture interspersed with pizzicato swirlings, pauses and breaks ; and to this the singer begins to add his warblings like a canary, with eyes half-closed, head thrown back and hands resting on his knees. Yes, he screeches like a bird ; he unsheathes his voice in a long, full-throated yell, which gets louder and louder, and is appallingly intense and protracted, as if, for a bet, he was trying to find out how

137

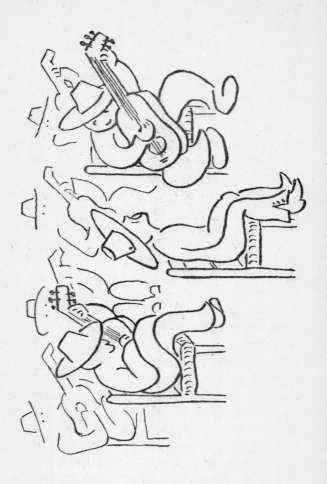

long he could keep it up with one breath ; suddenly this outstretched voice begins to quaver in a long trill, a protracted and piercing coloratura, which indulges in a tune of its own, performs a fluttering ripple, starts off on a queer, graceful meander, and suddenly sinks and dies away as the guitars chime in with a brisk strumming. And with their strains is joined and mingled this naked, shrill and rhetorical voice, bewailing its distress or whatever it is, in a passionate recitative, uncoiling sluggish and drunken from the abrupt rhythm of the guitars, and with one gasp swerving into that long, billowy vocal arabesque which dies away amid the clattering of the guitars. It is just like a shiny and flexible blade describing in the air luminous ripples and figures of eight ; it is also like the call of the muezzin and the enraptured strains of a canary chirping on its perch ; it is the dirge of the wilderness and, at the same time, a specimen of prodigious professional virtuosity ; it contains a great deal of natural gusto, of gipsyish hocus-pocus, a certain amount of Moorish artifice and untrammelled candour. It has nothing in common with the honeyed voices and the cooing of the Venetian gondoliers and the Neapolitan tricksters ; in Spain they shout at the top of their voices, harshly and frantically. The songs are generally filled with the woes of love, with taunts, jealousy and revenge ; they are a kind of epigram in one quatrain, set to music and prolonged by the wave of a slowly uncoiling, lingering trill. That is how they sing the

seguidillas, as well as the malagueñas, granadinas, tarantas, soleares, vidalitas, bulerías and other types of song, which differ from each other more in their contents than their form ; in fact, even the saetas, which are sung at Seville in the processions during the

Holy Week, have the same wild and passionate flamenco style as the amorous seguidilla.
Castañuelas : These are not only musical instruments which produce rattlings and drum-
   beats, trills, cooings and warblings—merely
   to keep up a rhythmic rattling is very diffi-

cult, as I know by experience—but also, and
particularly, dance instruments which make
the twirl of the dance pass into the fingers
and, just like a kettle-drum, raise the arms
in a sweeping curve above the head into that
splendid fundamental gesture of Spanish
dances.   The actual sound of the castañuelas

141

recalls darkest Africa with its frantic hankering after the rhythm of the drum-beat. When, during one of those whirlwind dances, the ear-splitting clatter of the castanets is heard amid piercing, provocative shouts and a rhythmical clapping of hands, then, dear reader, there is such a thrilling uproar, that it almost made me leap up and begin to caper riotously ; so violent is its effect upon feet and head.

Children : In the streets of Seville they dance a winsome measure, with one hand above the head and the other akimbo, the frock lifted for greater ease of movement ; a disdainful dance, with haughty shrugging gestures, and also a seemly dance. Little girls dancing in groups, miniature, doll-like figures of ballerinas, stamp their tiny heels and imitate the sultry and aggressive dance of the grown-up performers.

Erotic elements : Spanish dances cover the whole range of the erotic emotions, from amorous dalliance to orgasm ; but always, even in the most dignified quadrille, the erotic element is a trifle provocative ; it is not of that type which is displayed in the tango, but it excites, recoils and entices, challenges, threatens and slightly mocks. These are diabolical, amatory dances ; but they never lack a metallic mainspring of pride.

Fandango : This is danced in a dress with a

lengthy train ; to whirl round while wearing such a train, to kick it aside gracefully, to twirl like a top and stamp the heels—all this demands consummate skill and is a fine sight ; for this dance spurts up miraculously from a froth of flounces and lace petticoats.

Gipsy-girls : Most of them are from Triana ; for dancing they wear a long smock-like dress, which in olden times they used to lay aside ; and what they dance is in its essentials the cancan, the legs straddled and body bent back as far as the ground. The music

lashes the dancer on more and more feverishly, the protruding belly whirls more and more violently, navel and hips rotate, the hands writhe snakily, the heels are stamped defiantly, the body bends forward, as if it were struggling in the hands of a ruffian, a screech, and the gipsy-girl is sinking to the ground as if laid low by a spasm of bliss. It is a wild dance, boisterous and convulsive ; in it, sex, launching an attack, creeps, thrusts and parries ; the phallic cult of some formidable sect.

Gitanos : They dance, in pairs, a sexual pantomime of enticement and defiance, wooing and brutality ; they dance the traditional duet of man and woman, in which the woman is, if I may say so, a slut, and the man a ruffian who drags her along the ground. But if the gipsy dances by himself, he lays aside all pretext of pantomime ; then the thing becomes a sheer frenzy of movement, leapings and squattings, soaring gestures, and rabid stamping ; it is so genuine a dance that it expresses nothing else than liberated fire.

Guitar : The sounds it makes are utterly different from what we here imagine them to be ; it rings metallically like a cutlass, it rattles defiantly and harshly ; it does not growl, nor does it croon, coo or rustle, but it twangs like a bow-string, rumbles like a kettle-drum, clatters like sheet-iron ; it is a manly and boisterous instrument, played by fellows who look like mountain-brigands and who pluck at the strings with curt and jerky movements of the fingers.

Hija : ! Ole ! ! hija !

Chiquita : ¡ Bueno ! ¡ bueno ! chiquita.

Jota : The jota of Arragon is both a song and a dance ; a song with a heavy cadence, strange and harsh, which dashes on abruptly and then slackens, extremely Moorish, but without the flourishes which distinguish the flamenco ; each verse swerves suddenly into a protracted and drooping lamentation. And the jota is also a very attractive dance, swift and unfettered, with a jaunty, galloping rhythm which surges forth from the rounded slackening plain-song.

Muy : ¡ Bueno, chica ! ¡ Otra, otra !

Ole : ¡ Niña ! ¡ Ea !

Palmoteo : Or hand-clapping. While one of the group dances, the others sit around and beat time by clapping their hands, as if unable to hold out against the rhythmic eddy which is poured along in the cascading of the guitars. And they bawl. And they stamp their feet. And the guitar-players rock themselves to and fro on the chairs, stamp their feet and bawl. And on top of all this the castanets.

Rondalla : This is a fat-bellied mandoline of Arragon which produces a metallic and melodious clatter, and harmonizes with the tune of the iotas.

U : The U is a song of Valencia, the ecstatic scream of a singer amid the blare of trumpets and the feverish whirling of castanets ; never have I heard such a fervid singing as this long and appallingly tense yell of the Moors.

Zapatear : Or to stamp with a rhythmic gusto.

Bodega

SPAIN, like every old and worthy country, keeps up its regional peculiarities ; there are thousand and one differences between Valencia and Asturias, Arragon and Extremadura. Even nature has become associated with the localized patriotism which this involves, and produces a different sort of wine in each province. You must know that the wines of Castille promote valour, while the wines from the province of Granada arouse a grievous and frantic sorrow, and the wines of Andalusia induce feelings of delight and cheerfulness ; the wines from Rioja refresh the mind, the Catalan wines endow the tongue with adroitness, and the wines of Valencia sink to the heart.

You must know, too, that the sherry which is drunk on the spot where it is made, does not resemble the sweetened sherry which we drink ; it is light in colour, pungently flavoured with a bitterish tartness, soft as oil, but heady all the same, for it is a sea-coast wine. Brown Malaga is thick and sticky, like fragrant honey, in which a fiery sting is hidden. And then there is a goodly wine called Manzanilla of San Lucar ; as its name shows, it is a young and exuberant wine, worldly and jovial ; when you have quaffed your fill of

Manzanilla, you float along buoyantly as a skiff in a good wind.

You must know also that each province has

different sorts of fish and different sorts of cheese, as well as different sorts of sausage and saveloy, beans and melons, olives and grapes, sweetmeats

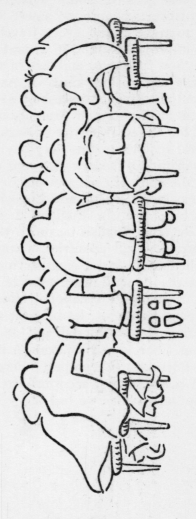

and other local gifts of God. That is why the old and trustworthy authors assert that it is instructive to travel ; and every traveller whose aim it is to improve his mind in distant lands will assure you how precious and essential a thing good victuals are. The kings of Asturias are no more, but the smoked cheese of Asturias still survives ; the palmy days of Aranjuez are a thing of the past, but the strawberries of Aranjuez enjoy their historic renown to this very day. Do not be gluttons or finicky feeders ; let your meals be a homage to the gods of time and place. I should like to eat caviare in Russia and English bacon in England ; but, alas, in England I was given caviare to eat, and English bacon in the land of Spain. Patriots of all countries, a conspiracy is being hatched against us ; neither international finance nor the Fourth Internationale is such a menace to us as the International Hotel-Keeper. I implore you, caballeros, let us fight against his wiles, uttering sundry sacred and ancient war-cries, such as Chorizo, Kalbshaxen, A la lanterne, Macaroni, Porridge, Camembert, Pereat, Manzanilla and many others, according to where we are and how pugnacious we feel.

Carabela

IT is anchored on the Guadalquivir near that
Torre del Oro, where the Spanish ships used
to unload Peruvian gold ; and it is said to be an
exact model, to the last plank and rope, of the
carabela Santa Maria on which Christopher
Columbus discovered America. I went to have
a look at it in the hope that, as a result, something
would occur to me on the subject of Christopher
Columbus ; I went right through it, from the
lower deck to the top ; I lay down on the bed in
the cabin of Columbus, and as a souvenir I took
a number of *La Vanguardia* which was lying on
the table there, apparently another relic of
Columbus ; I meddled with the falconetas or
culebrinas or whatever they call those old cannons,
during which process I nearly broke my leg with
an iron bullet, for they were loaded ; but I discovered nothing except my own astonishment
at finding the famous ship so small. I doubt
whether the Port of London authority would
allow it to be used for passenger traffic as far as
Tilbury.

But up on deck I remembered that behind me
was the Ibero-American Exhibition ; and when
it was closed, its existence would be perpetuated

by a large Ibero-American University which, so we Sevillanos hope, will be attended by young caballeros from Mexico and Guatemala, Argentine and Peru and Chile. At that moment I felt terribly anxious to be a Spanish patriot and to exult aloud, thus : Hombres, just consider that yonder, on the other side of the ocean, there are millions and millions of people who speak a

language in accordance with the dictionary of the Madrid Academy. Now although the countries there are as plentiful as blackberries, there is only one nation, and if we were to set about the job properly, there would be only one civilization, too, ¿ sabe ? I imagine, caballeros, what would happen if all people who kept to the dictionary of the Madrid Academy were to throw in their lot together ; this would immediately produce something which not even the League of Nations has managed to bring about—a

Euroamerica, an inter-continental alliance of the white race. Why, this would be like a new discovery of America. Just fancy how we Iberians would open the eyes of those Great Powers with their everlasting disputes about tonnage and calibre! Amigos, every estranjero, who trots into our country by way of Irún or Portbu, only has to glance round and he at once notices that of old we Spaniards showed signs of greatness and supremacy; where, by all that's holy, has it gone to? In the name of Goya and Cervantes, let us get back to it!

That and in like manner is how I would speak to them; for when you are standing on a vessel which recalls the carabela of Columbus, you feel a sort of compulsion to discover America. I did not discover America, but in this country I discovered something closer to us; I think it is called nationalism. What I mean is that this nation, more than any other—not counting the English— has succeeded in preserving its own peculiar mode of life; from the women's mantillas to the music of Albéniz, from the household usages to the street traders, from the caballeros to the donkeys, it prefers its old Spanish manners to the veneer of international civilization. This may be due to the climate, or to the fact that the country is almost an island; but first and foremost it is a question of character. Here local pride makes every caballero hold his head high; the Gaditano glories in being a man of Cadiz, and the Madrileno

in being a man of Madrid ; the Asturian is proud
to be a man of Asturia, and the Castillan is proud

in general ; for each of these names has the renown
of an escutcheon.   In consequence of which, the

Sevillan, I hope, will never demean himself so far as to become a good international European ; for he would not become even a Madrileno. One of the deeper secrets of Spain is its provincialism, a peculiar virtue which, in the rest of Europe, is dying out ; a provincialism which is the joint product of nature, history and people. Spain has not yet ceased to be in close touch with nature, and has still not lost sight of its history ; that is why it has managed to preserve itself to such an extent. And all that the rest of us can do is to observe, with a certain amount of wonder, how fine a thing it is to be a nation.

Palmas y Naranjos

HAVING travelled through the La Mancha region in a night as dark as a gipsy, I cannot say whether it really contains giants or whether they are merely wind-mills ; but on the other hand I can enumerate to you quite a lot of things which are to be found in the provinces of Murcia and Valencia, to wit and particularly : yellow or red rocks, white crags of limestone and blue hills as a background ; on each rock, crag and hill the ruins of a Moorish fortress or a Christian stronghold or at least a hermitage, a chapel or a belfry ; the huge brown remains of Montesa, the citadel of Játiva bristling with towers and battlements, all kinds of fortifications, fortresses and watchtowers ; the stronghold of Puig and the ramparts of Nules, the ruins of Sagunto, a whole acropolis on a rocky summit, and the four-square castle of Benicarló ;

brown and red wastes of rocky hill-sides, overgrown with tufts of esparto, with hazel-bushes, sprays of thyme, rosemary, tenkria and sage ; arid slopes parched like pottery just removed from the oven and still hot ; and right below them

olive gardens, grey and silvery, similar to our willows, with their gnarled and twisted trunks

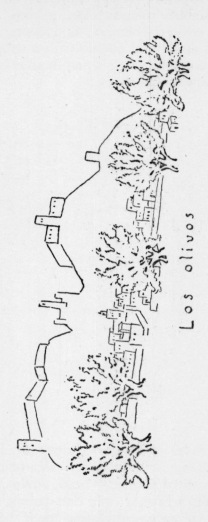

Los olivos

which resemble mandragoras, goblins or something else remotely human ; and among the olives a parched and stony puebla with a small church like a stronghold, with squat houses and some sort of large ruins above ;

Las palmas

then, groves of fig-trees, large-leaved and unkempt ; dense and luxuriant algarobias, which produce pods of the carob-bean, otherwise known as St. John's bread ; and date-palms, rows upon rows of palms thrusting their triumphant tops aloft ; palm-groves, townships steeped in palms, glistening faience cupolas and minarets amid palms and banana-trees, and above this another stronghold of some sort or other ;

irrigated huertas, rice-fields, mulberry plantations, stretches of vineyards and acres of orange-trees, small and round with tough, glossy leaves

Los naranjos

and oranges arraying themselves in golden tints, and lemon-trees which are larger and more like pear-trees ; a land flowing with milk and honey, if ever I saw one, tierras de regadio where the fertilizing moisture still flows through gutters and runnels which were laid down by Roman farmers and Moorish architects ; and above this golden land, on the blue hills, bastions, turrets and notched walls of Moorish strongholds ;

Valencia, with its blue and gold azulejo cupolas,

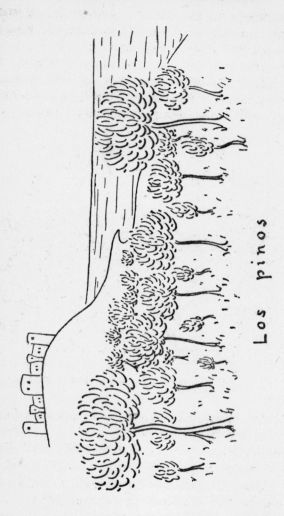

Los pinos

its brown-faced people and golden air, in which sea-air and the smell of fish is mingled with the fragrance of oranges and syrup;

sea, sea, sea luminous, flaming, opalescent and crinkled, foaming at the foot of brown rocks, licking the sandy beaches, and azure sea, sea whose range baffles the eye; malarial lagoons, inlets

Los alcornoques

amid the rocks, the wing-shaped sail of a fishing boat on the horizon;

alcornoques, groves of cork-oaks with leaves which are almost black, leathery and coiled into the shape of pointed paper-bags; small pine-groves on the salt sandy flats; on the mountains strongholds and hermitages;

so the sea on the right, and on the left, mountains—where must I look so as to leave nothing out ?—oh, to float on the sea or to be a hermit on yonder mountains,

to sail out on a fishing cruise, to tread grapes or to press out oil, ha, you scarlet rocks, nowhere are rocks so crimson,

behold, Oropesa, a township clinging to a rock, doubtless it looked exactly the same a thousand years ago, although I cannot tell what nation dwelt there then ;

whenever you ride through a tunnel, it is as if you had put a full stop and the beginning of a new chapter followed it,

—and yet you could not say at what point the country undergoes such a change, or in what the change consists ; suddenly it reminds you of something else. It is no longer Africa, but something familiar to you ; it might be the Corniche at Marseilles or the Riviera di Levante ; once more it is Latin country, the warm and sparkling Mediterranean basin, and when you look at the map, you discover that it is called Cataluña.

Tibidabo

TIBIDABO is a hill above Barcelona ; on the top there is a church, cafés and swings, and especially a view of the sea, the town and its surroundings ; the sea in question gleams with a steamy haze, the town emits an uncommonly delicate sparkle of white dwellings, and its surroundings are tinged with a green and pink lustre.

Or from the Font del Lleó terrace, there is beauty for you, the shining town between the warm surge of the hills and the sea, a vista as stimulating as light wine.

Or evening on the slope of Montjuich at the exhibition, when all the fountains, conduits and cascades, the frontages and turrets are set agleam with such an array of lights that you are at a loss to describe it, and all you can do is to look at it till your head begins to whirl.

But these fabulous items are incomplete without Barcelona itself ; a rich city, as good as new, which rather flaunts its money, its industries, its new streets, shops and villas ; there are miles and miles of them, left and right, and in the middle, as if at the bottom of a pocket, the old town manages to wedge itself in around a few ancient and venerable objects, such as a cathedral, a town hall and a Diputación, with its close and swarming streets, cut in two by the famous Rambla, where the populace of Barcelona jostles under the plane-trees to buy flowers, to ogle the girls and to start revolutions. All in all, a brisk and pleasant city, blazoning forth its prosperity, rushing out to the surrounding hills, an ostentatious and flamboyant place, like its fanciful architect

Gaudi, who so feverishly elevated his soul heavenward in the unfinished nave and the pine-cone turrets of that vast cathedral torso, Sagrada Familia.

And the harbour, dirty and noisy like all harbours, an enclosed zone of nocturnal resorts, dancing halls and shows, filled at nightfall with the clatter and the racket of all their mechanical orchestras, blatant with coloured lights, gross and rampant with its queer mob of stevedores, seamen, riffraff, plump wenches, rowdies and harbour dregs, a brothel larger than Marseilles,

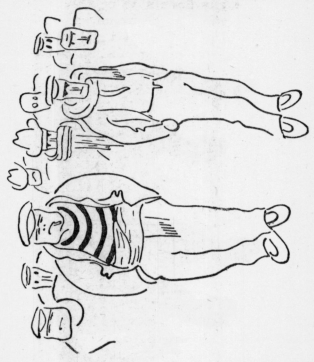

a low haunt more dubious than Limehouse, a sink of iniquity where earth and sea shed their scum.

And the working-class suburbs, where you see men with their clenched fists in their pockets, and

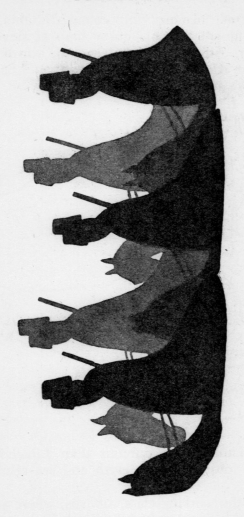

rabid, defiant eyes ; let me tell you, this is very different from the free and easy dwellers in Triana ; take a sniff, and you will discover that something is smouldering here. At nightfall shadows range along towards the centre of the town ; they wear espadrillas on their feet and red belts round their waists ; a cigarette clings to their lips and their caps are pulled down over their eyes. They are only shadows, but when you look round, they form quite a cluster. A cluster of staring, dogged eyes.

And here, in the middle of the city, are people who refuse to be Spaniards ; and in the mountains round about, peasants who are not Spaniards. From the heights of Tibidabo it is a brilliant and prosperous city ; but as you get nearer and nearer to it, you seem to hear the sound of rapid panting between clenched teeth.

Meanwhile, Barcelona overflows with lights and amuses itself hectically ; the theatres do not open till midnight, at two in the morning the dancing halls and other pleasure haunts are packed ; the silent and sullen clusters loiter on the ramblas and paseos, and suddenly, noisily disappear when an equally silent and sullen posse of mounted gendarmes, with rifles ready in the saddle, come into view at the next corner.

Sardana

BUT, Catalonians, I would rather you played your sardana to me, that shrill and forthright musical instrument, the sound of which combines the bleating of a goat with the whistling of a shawm—real Mediterranean music. This is not

the straggling yell of the Moors nor the dark passion of the guitars ; it is rural, uncouth and cheerful like this region itself.

For here the country now resembles Provence ; thus, it is not as rocky as the rest of Spain, but as the Provençal hills ; no palms grow there like those in Murcia, but the palms that grow there are like those on the Riviera. As you notice, the distinction is a subtle one, and is not easy to put into words ; it is in the air you breathe, it is in the people and their dwellings with the green shutters, but, above all, it just simply is.

As regards the inhabitants of this region, they wear on their feet white woven slippers called

alpargatas, which remind you of Roman sandals ; and here and there you come across red Phrygian caps (they are called barretinas or something of that sort). And many of them are blue-eyed and brown-haired, thickset and stocky ; somehow a touch of the north has got into everything here, the music, the taste of the wine, the people and the natural features. The majority of the trees are deciduous ; the first yellow leaf of a plane-

tree which I saw was like a greeting from home. The people do not live in patios as they do yonder, but in the streets ; children and dogs and mothers, topers and newspaper-readers, mules and cats, they all live on the doorstep and on the pavement; perhaps that is why in this country it is so easy for a mob to form and street-fights to start.

But if I must say what surprised me most, it was the gendarmes in front of the royal castle; for they wear white Catalan slippers on their feet and a top-hat on their heads. You see, a top-hat, slippers, and a rifle with fixed bayonet, is a peculiar and unusual combination; but, after all, it graphically represents the character of the Catalan country, a rural and commercial area among the other kingdoms of Spain.

Pelota

PELOTA is a Basque game with a hard ball made of dogskin. From a distance it looks as if a shindy had just started and that the noise of shooting was being added to the wild uproar; but when you get nearer, you discover that the

uproar is not caused by the players or even by the onlookers but by the betting-touts, who rush about in front of the crowd and take bets on Blue or Red, these being the distinctive colours of the teams. From a dramatic point of view these betting-touts are the most interesting feature of the show; for they yell like monkeys, leap about, wave their arms and indicate the bets on their outstretched fingers, the bets and winnings

being flung to and fro between touts and onlookers in hollow pellets, which whizz past your nose like nuts shaken from a tree where a gang of apes are squatting.

While this passionate betting-game is developing, the pelota in the narrow sense of the word is being played lower down in front of the crowd. On each side there are two players with a sort of long wicker pod or trough, fastened to the right hand by means of a leather glove. Elola catches the flying ball in this pod, and wallop,

he swipes it against the high wall which is known as the fronton. The ball bounces off with a crash, and whizzes back with the momentum of a projectile ; bang, now Gabriel has got it in his pod, and shoots it against the wall. Houp-la, now Ugalde has collared it from the air into his pod, whirls the racket round, and flings the ball at the fronton like a bomb. And bang, now Teodoro has got it in his trough and whacks it against the wall with a thud ; now it is Elola's turn again to catch it as it bounces off. That is what it looks like in terms of a slow-motion film; but in reality you see four white figures, each leaping in his line, and smack bang, smack bang, smack bang, the ball flies above them and remains almost invisible; if the player misses it, if the ball bounces on the ground twice, or if some other

mysterious slip is made, that ends the round and the other team scores one point; the touts begin to wave their arms and with a terrific yell announce fresh bets. And so it goes on until sixty points or thereabouts have been scored. Then a fresh set of Rojos and Azules arrive, and they begin all over again, while the crowd is re-shuffled, as if they were so many roulette-players.

As you see, it has all the attributes of a mono-tonous game, especially when we use such elementary and common phrases as " catching the ball " ; but in reality the process is not one of catching, but involves rather a species of magic. The pod, known as *la cesta*, is no more than a hand's breadth across, and the ball flies at about

the same speed as a meteor ; apparently on a recent occasion it bounced off the wall and flew among the onlookers, whereupon all four players took to their heels, as they felt sure that the ball must have killed someone in the crowd. So to catch a ball like that is very much like catching in a spoon a bullet from a rifle ; and the pelota-players catch every ball wherever it may hurtle, with the same dead certainty as that with which a swift catches flies. They just stretch out their arms, and they've got it. They just take a leap, and they've got it. Compared to pelota, tennis is like chasing flies with a fly-clapper. And on top of all that, they perform their tricks, the leaps and the somersaults, without any display or exertion, very much like a bird hunting gnats. There's a bang, the ball crashes against the wall,

and the thing's done ; not a sign of the brawny strength with which it must have been hurled. That's the sort of game it is, queer and monotonous.

This game is played only by the Basques and the men from the hills of Navarre ; the Basques, who have introduced to the world the beret (they call it *boina*) ; the Basques, who, as Professor Meillet informed me, are the original inhabitants of the whole Mediterranean basin, and akin to certain tribes of the Caucasus. Their language is so complex that it has not yet been fully investigated ; and they make their music with a clarinet

reed-pipe, called *dulzaina*, accompanied by a
small drum. They are one of the tiniest nations

in Europe, perhaps they are what is left of the
vanished people of Atlantis. It would be a
crime if this dauntless remnant also vanished.

Montserrat

SEEN from a distance, it is a sturdy, impressive mountain which, from the waist upwards, overtops the other hills of Catalonia; but the nearer you get to it, the more are you amazed, and you shake your head, till at last all you can do is to mutter: " Well, I'm hanged ! " and " I've never seen anything like that before." Which only goes to confirm the old experience that the things of this world are more remarkable at close quarters than from afar.

For, you see, what from Barcelona looks like a compact range turns out at close quarters to be a mountain perched on columns; in fact, it looks more like a specimen of ecclesiastical architecture than a mountain. Below, there is a plinth of red rock, from which rocky pillars tower upwards; on top of them there is something resembling a gallery which supports a fresh row of huge columns; and above them a third storey of this immense colonnade hoists itself upwards to a height of more than six thousand feet. Well, I'm hanged; I must say, I've never seen anything like that before. The higher the fine spiral path uncoils, the more it makes you hold your breath; below, the steep precipice of Llobregat and above your head the steep towers of Montserrat ; and between the two, as if it were on a projecting balcony, hangs a holy monastery and a cathedral and a garage for several hundred cars, motor-buses and charabancs, together with a hostel where you can

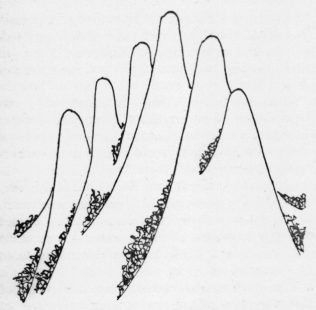

lodge with the Benedictine monks in that monumental and bristling hermitage ; and in this monastery there is a library such as perhaps no other monastery contains, which ranges from old folios in wooden and pigskin bindings, to a whole shelf of books about cubism.

But there is still the peak of the mountain,

Sant Jeroni ; you are taken there by an absolutely vertical funicular railway, which makes you think of a sardine-tin being hauled along a rope to the top of a church-steeple ; but you take your seat in this tin, and try to look alert and adventurous, as if you were not frightened out of your wits at the possibility of being hurled to kingdom come. And when you get to the top and pull yourself together, you do not know what you ought to look at first ; so I will draw up a list of things for you :

1. The vegetation which, seen from below, looks like tufts of hair under the armpits of those huge upraised limbs, but at close quarters it proves to be a delightful crop of evergreen barberries and holly, box-tree and spindle-tree, rock-rose, myrtle and laurel and Mediterranean heather ; I'll be hanged if I've ever seen such a natural park as here on the mountain-top and among the crevices in these expanses of hard rubble which look as if they were moulded from flinty concrete.

2. The towers and columns of the rocks of Montserrat, the naked, awe-inspiring steeps of the Evil Valley, which is supposed to have split apart on the day of Christ's crucifixion. There are a number of scientific theories as to what these rocks resemble ; according to some, they are like sentries, according to others, a procession of monks in cowls, or flutes, or roots of extracted teeth. I myself call heaven to witness that they

resemble upraised fingers clutched together as in prayer ; and so Montserrat prays with a thousand

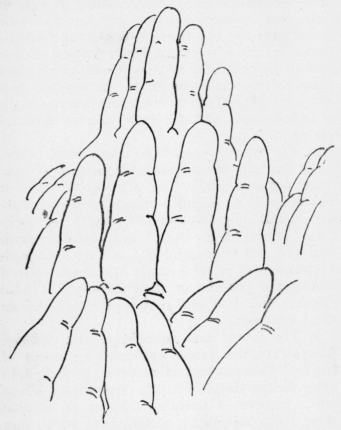

fingers, avows with lifted forefingers, blesses the pilgrims and makes a sign. My own belief is that it was created and upraised above all other

mountains for this special purpose, and my belief is further, that it is now out of place, but I thought of this while sitting on the summit of Sant Jeroni, which forms the highest peak and, at the same time, the centre of this vast and quaint natural cathedral.

3. And then there is the surrounding country, earth rippling, farther than the eye can reach, in green and pink heights : Cataluña, Navarra, Arragon ; the Pyrenees with sparkling glaciers ; white townships at the foot of the mountains ; queer, oval hills, so arranged as to look like ruffled tresses through which a huge comb has been passed. Or rather, they look as if they were still marked by the furrowed imprint of the fingers which created this land. From the summit of Montserrat you see the imprint of the divine thumbs which kneaded this warm, russet region with a special creative zest.

Having beheld all this and marvelled thereat, the pilgrim set out on his homeward journey.

Vuelta

THE homeward journey. I have to travel across four countries yet, but whatever I see now, absent-mindedly I let slip between my fingers like the beads of a rosary ; for now it is

España

only the way back. A man who is returning home, squeezes himself into a corner of the railway-carriage, and half-closes his eyes ; enough,

enough of this passing-by and withdrawing;
enough of all these places which slip away almost
as soon as they have beckoned. All he wants
now is to be home again, like a post fixed into
the ground; to see around him, morning and
evening, the same familiar things. Yes, but the
world is such a large place!

France

Just look at the fellow and see what a fool he
is! There he sits in the corner like a bundle of
misery, and he is annoyed because he did not
see more of it. He hasn't seen Salamanca or
Santiago; he hasn't encountered the king of the
gipsies, nor heard the sound of the Basque
txistularis. He ought to see all and stretch out

his hand towards everything, just as he patted that donkey at Toledo or stroked the trunk of the palm in the garden of the Alcazar. He ought at least to touch everything with his fingers. To pass the palm of his hand across the whole world. What a delight it is, dear reader, to see or to handle something which, till then, was unfamiliar

Belaïque

to you. Each divergency in things and people widens the bounds of life.

With gratitude and joy you have gleaned everything that differed from what you were accustomed to ; and whatever other pilgrims you saw, were willing to walk themselves off their feet to make sure of not missing anything special and picturesque and different from what they could see elsewhere ; for in us all there is a love for the fullness and teeming of life. Now this fullness of life is brought about by nations ; of course, by history and environment as well, but the two are merged in nations. So if it ever occurred to

D . R

us to let the affairs of this world be controlled by a love of life, we should have to say something of this sort (in all the languages of the world) :

Caballeros, it is true of course, that people are people, all the world over, but what caused us travellers such a pleasant surprise was not so much

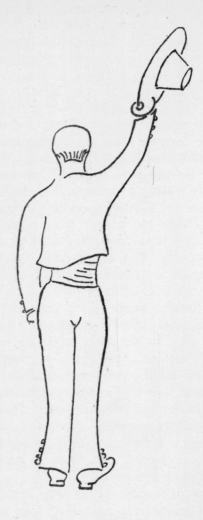

the discovery that, for instance, the Sevillans are people, as the discovery that the Sevillans are Sevillans. We were delighted to find that the Spaniards really are Spaniards ; the more Spanish they were, the more we liked them and the more highly we thought of them. Bear in mind that we should think just as highly of the Chinese for the exciting reason that they are Chinese, of the Portuguese because they are Portuguese, and we do not understand a word they say. And so on. There are people who love the whole world as long as it is willing to have asphalt high-roads or to believe in one God or to close the bodegas and taverns. There are people who could love the world if only it would assume just their own single civilized aspect. But as we have not yet made much progress with love, let us try another way. It is far more delightful to be fond of the world because it has thousands of aspects and is different everywhere, and then to announce : Friends, as we are so glad to see each other, let us make a League of Nations ; but hang it, they must be Nations with all the proper trimmings, each one with different hair and a different language, well, its own customs and culture, and if need be, with all right, with its own God, too ; for every divergence deserves to be cherished, simply because it widens the bounds of life. Let us be united by everything that divides us !

And here, the man on his way home, lets his eyes nestle against the vine-clad hills of France, lets them fondle the hop-fields of Germany, and with feverish delight looks forward to seeing the tilled land and the apple-orchards beyond the last frontier.